Embodied POWER

Tara Jackson

Copyright © 2025 by Tara Jackson

All rights reserved. No part of this publication may be reproduced, distributed or transmitted in any form or by any means without permission of the publisher, except in the case of brief quotations referencing the body of work and in accordance with copyright law.

The information given in this book should not be treated as a substitute for professional medical advice; always consult a medical practitioner. Any use of information in this book is at the reader's discretion and risk. Neither the author nor the publisher can be held responsible for any loss, claim or damage arising out of the use, or misuse, of the suggestions made, the failure to take medical advice or for any material on third party websites.

ISBN:
978-1-916529-71-7 (Paperback)
978-1-916529-72-4 (ebook)

Cover design by Lynda Mangoro.

The Unbound Press
www.theunboundpress.com

Hey unbound one!

Welcome to this magical book brought to you by The Unbound Press.

At The Unbound Press we believe that when women write freely from the fullest expression of who they are, it can't help but activate a feeling of deep connection and transformation in others. When we come together, we become more and we're changing the world, one book at a time!

This book has been carefully crafted by both the author and publisher with the intention of inspiring you to move ever more deeply into who you truly are.

We hope that this book helps you to connect with your Unbound Self and that you feel called to pass it on to others who want to live a more fully expressed life.

With much love,

Nicola Humber

Founder of The Unbound Press
www.theunboundpress.com

For all the younger versions of me.

CONTENTS

A note on who this book is for	11
Preface: how this book came to be	13

Let's begin — **23**

For the ones who've never *really* fit in	28
The golden pool	30
The dragons	32
Messages from the elemental power dragons	33

Embodied Power — **35**

Feeling power-less	37
Become who you came here to be	41
Embodied Power	42
The power of you	44
Re-writing power	45
This is what power is to me...	47
Welcoming your power	48
The power in BE-ing in a body	50
Fear of your own power	52
Giving away your power	54
I trust my power	56
The power in rage	57
I've always known this...	59
You GET to do this	61
Your power is medicine	62
The codes you carry	63

Earth: Embodied Love — **65**

BE-ing on Earth	67
The Earth is creative power	68
Commit to being on Earth	69

An ode to my body	70
Put it all down for a moment	72
Let it be messy	74
A moment of pause	75
Being held	76
Claiming your body sovereignty	78
Chords of resonance	81
'Dark' powers	82
Opening up to a full sensory experience	84
Choosing yourself	86
The power in the past	88
Nourish your roots	91
Do-ing drama	93
Who you really are	94
The vulnerability in being fully you	95
You are magnificent	97
Water: Embodied Money	**99**
Money, money, money	101
Dancing with money	103
Your money roots	104
Musing with the energy of money	106
A date with money	109
Trusting money	111
Feeling safe to let money in	114
How do you want to feel?	116
Body beliefs	117
Cancelling contracts, cords and commitments	122
The codes of money	124
What do you make money mean?	126
The gift of money	127
Take responsibility	128
The link between money and water	129
The frequency of money	131
Follow the flow	133
The cyclical nature of money	134
The Earth's money	135

Wisdom from Gaia	138
New to money	140
Money wants to be told...	143
Money wants you to know...	144
Keep believing	145
I AM money	146
Magical money	147

Air: Embodied Magic — 149

The girl who remembered her magic	151
Claiming your magical powers	154
Tending to your magic	155
Intuitive magic	156
When it doesn't make sense	159
Timeline jumping	161
It's time to come out of hiding	164
Alchemising the past	165
Returning what's Hers	166
Root remembering	168
The heart of the root	169
Unlocking the magical codes of your ancestry	170
The heart lock	171
The power in words	172
Get out of your own way	174
Playing with time	176
Re-wiring your system	177
Water whispering	178
Morphogenic fields	179
Energetic protection of your spaces	181
Chakra dragon clearing	183
Knowing it is done	185
Magical tools	187
Have fun with your magic	190
Embodied magic	191
Receiving consent	193

Fire: Embodied Leader	**195**
My leadership today	197
What is leadership?	199
You came here with a frequency	200
The time of the visionary, creative leader is here	201
You are the formula	202
The leader's journey	204
Disruptors, rebels and change-makers	205
Bridging the worlds	206
Embrace the paradox	207
Softening into your power as a gentle leader	208
Letting the mystery lead	210
What if you couldn't get it wrong?	213
Tug of war	214
It's never going to be perfect	215
Know when it's time to let go	216
When you enter the void	217
Receiving from the void	220
Seeking external validation	221
Your circle of support	223
Trust the pace of your becoming	225
The power of energetic containers	227
What if being fully you is key?	228
Getting to know the little leader inside	229
What's stopping you?	231
When the critics come out	232
Small acts of care	234
Embodied visibility	236
How are you being called to share?	240
You came here to freaking radiate	242
Embodied impact	244
Who are you really?	246
Become the leader you are here to be	248
Embodied leader	249
A portal into your power	250
Let's go deeper	251

Resources   252

Further resources and ways to connect with me	252
Working with limiting beliefs	255
Overview of the main chakras	257
Chakras diagram	259
Acknowledgements	260
About The Author	261

A NOTE ON WHO THIS BOOK IS FOR

This book is for the visionaries, mystics, seers, sensitives, healers; for all those who know, deep down, that they're here to lead in their own unique way.

It's for those who've never quite fit in. (Spoiler alert: you're not meant to fit in. That's your gift.) Yes, you are damn good at masking, like a chameleon you're able to change and blend in to belong. But it's likely created a lot of inner tension and compartmentalising, and left you exhausted at times.

It's for the ones who were called crazy, weird, or a loser, because you saw the world differently from the majority. You receive the nuances more acutely. You still do. You see what's needed. You see solutions to possibilities. Ways that could re-write the old. You are here to create the new. You are here to make an impact in your unique way.

You are ready to own your creative energy and reclaim your power to consciously shape your life and your leadership.

It's for magical, spiritual beings who are a bridge between the worlds. You have a mission here on Earth and know that to live it fully, you must be fully yourself.

You care about the planet. You care about other humans and all other life-forms and know we're all connected. You are aware this is a pivotal point on Earth and that we are creating for the generations to come.

A small caveat: After working with many people on reclaiming their power, and through my own experience, I've learned that stepping into true power (being fully yourself in the world, unapologetically and unashamedly expressed) often requires deep self-knowing and a willingness to heal, or at least move through, what's been holding you back.

If you sense there's still some foundational inner work to do – and you're not quite ready to explore this alone or with support – this book might not be the right companion just yet.

Ultimately though, power is for everyone! And if you're drawn to this book, I trust there's something here for you. So feel free to dive straight in. I hope it supports you :-)!

PREFACE: HOW THIS BOOK CAME TO BE

I wanted to share the story of how this book came to be, as originally I thought it was going to be a book about money. In fact I initially committed to write a book called *Embodied Money* in September 2023, and that's the journey I set out on.

To give you a little context, especially if you're new to my world: I work intimately with the energy or spirit of every creation I bring into being, whether it's a book, an offering, a course, or a piece of art. I co-create by attuning to its energetic essence, receiving its guidance, and letting it guide and co-create with me. If you're curious about this process, I've written a whole book on it: *Embodied Creation*.

So, when I began this new project – *Embodied Money* – my intention was clear. I wanted to transform my relationship with money. I longed for the kind of consistent five-figure-plus months so many in the entrepreneurial world aim for. I wanted financial growth year on year. I wanted to be one of *those* people. The ones who no longer had to think about money, who received abundantly without worry or fluctuation. I wanted to be done with the cycle of feast and famine: months of comfort followed by months of scraping by.

Deep down, I knew something had to shift. Writing this book felt like a way to catalyse that change. A part of me also knew, from writing previous books, that each one is a portal, an initiation. The embodiment of its wisdom begins the moment I commit to writing it. Why would this one be any different?

Well, here's what happened.

After committing to writing this book (which for me included saying 'yes' to the journey it was going to take me on. Fully surrendering to being a co-creator with THE essence of the book that *really* wanted to be written, in spite of my original intentions. Plus anything else that might come up on the journey), its essence vanished.

The energy of the book I had strongly been feeling (which was fierce and fast, with a sparkly, yet get-shit-done vibe) was gone. It's as though the book had sent a messenger out into the world to find someone ready and willing to write it, and then once I put my hand up, its mission was complete, so it left.

From this new place, I kept trying to connect to the essence of the book, secretly wanting... hoping... praying to feel all of this deep, fast alchemy for how to magically transform my financial situation overnight. But nope, that's not what came. Instead it felt like a deep, powerful, rumble from right inside the centre of the Earth. Two golden dragons spiralled up from the centre of this vortex, threading themselves through the ancient ley lines that pulse beneath the land where I live.

The more I tried to receive clarity or next steps, the quieter it all became. This new energy required space. Stillness. Time. More space. More time. It asked me to *create* time and space in my life. So I did. Truthfully, I don't think I had much choice. I resisted, still grasping for something to *do*, still hoping the book would drop me the answers. But that's not how it unfolded.

During this liminal phase, sitting with the soul of the book, I began painting and feeling into the emotional landscape that was surfacing around money. What came up was raw and wide-reaching: childhood memories, beliefs, traumas, triggers, even past life echoes. I let these energies move through me via painting and a method called neurographic art – an intuitive way of making the unconscious conscious through flowing forms.

The first active bit of guidance I received from the book was to do 33 days of yin yoga (which quickly became 66). My first reaction? "WTAF does this have to do with money?" But I'm not one to ignore the guidance of a book. And if nothing else, it gave me something to *do* (ahh, the illusion of doing). So I followed it.

As I began the daily yin practice, the book guided me to start talking to my body about money. Allowing my body to signal to me the part that wanted to speak that day. There was no pushing, no forcing, simply getting into my body, with curiosity, seeing what wanted to emerge. It made no logical sense whatsoever. It's only in hindsight do I see what was actually happening, and how it was bringing me deeper into the wisdom of my body.

Alongside this I felt a deep calling to connect to roots of all kinds. My roots: through my ancestry (in India as I am adopted from there), the roots of trees and other vegetation, my root chakra, my childhood roots, and some past lives. I spent a lot of time connecting to the Earth, breathing into and painting roots. Again, I went with it, but had no idea what it was guiding me into.

Then, in classic human fashion, I decided to take some kind of control. I turned to mindset work – surely *this* was the missing piece. I dusted off the dozens of money courses I'd accumulated over the years, convinced I still had more belief work to do. I even bought a couple more with what little money I had left, hoping I would finally find something to help me clear my blocks. But nothing substantial came.

So I took action – serious, focused action. I created new workshops, both online and in person. I entered my first art exhibition in years to sell some of my paintings. I ran a free online immersion: a strategy that had previously worked brilliantly in my business. I started showing up daily on social media, promoting my books, courses, offerings. I did *all* the things I knew to do.

And... barely anything happened.

I enrolled three people into my membership at a nominal rate. I sold one painting, and that was to my parents (who didn't realise it was mine). All that energy, all that action, and it felt like nothing in return.

I was devastated. Disheartened. I wanted to throw in the towel, scrap the book, shut down the business. But deep inside, I *knew*. I knew that I had been taking action from misalignment. That the true guidance was not about doing more. It was about going deeper. I had ignored that still, wise voice in favour of old business tactics that once worked, but no longer did.

You might be reading this thinking, "You didn't try very hard – you only took action for a short amount of time, of course it didn't shift anything, you should have kept going." I hear you; you have a fair point. That's how most businesses operate: consistent effort, visible results. But something inside me knew this wasn't the path. At least not right then. There was another way calling me, and because I've chosen to co-create with Spirit, I knew I had to listen.

Then my business income almost completely dried up. For almost five months.

The clients I thought I had for at least another six months at least, decided to leave early. The ones that were staying had already paid, so that money had been accounted for. There was nothing else coming in, except a trickle from the membership and the odd item in my web shop. We're talking less than $50 a month.

I hit my financial rock bottom in my business. I felt like such a failure. Maybe I should write a book about how to **not** make money... Yet, during that time – I was completely and utterly supported, more than ever before. Abundantly in fact. My nourishing organic meals were paid for, my transport and entrance to the beautiful forest where I walk was covered. I even received the opportunity to work with an incredible coach – all fully paid for.

I am deeply aware of my privilege and am profoundly grateful to my friends, my family, and especially my partner. The level of safety, care and support I experienced changed something in me. For good...

I know I am not alone here – so many people I have spoken to (maybe you too) have worked on their money beliefs and more, and then gone through phases of not having much, or even any income from their own efforts. Yet they look back on these times and are SO fully held and supported. Everything is provided for, somehow. Miraculously there's always just enough money.

I started to let go. I started to let myself be supported. I stopped judging my inadequacy at not being able to receive money consistently through my business in the same way as others – the way I thought it needed to be. I then started to let the book *really* talk to me, without expectation or forcing it to be something I thought it should be.

This is when the book and I opened to a new, much deeper relationship. It took me into my body into my energy centres (my chakras specifically) like never before. And simultaneously, it took me beyond the Earth, to places I couldn't have imagined. Through visions, colours, images and energetic journeys. I could feel myself shifting and changing from the inside out. I felt like I was being re-born, re-coded and re-calibrated all at the same time.

This is where I began to understand, and receive a glimpse into, the true magic of what this book was here to hold.

It started as I normally do when working with a creative idea – walking with the spirit of the book in nature. But, rather than being a conversation or connection with the energy, which is the norm for me, instead I was immediately guided to start calling down Source energy and clearing my chakras from the root up to the crown.

If you aren't familiar with the chakras (which are energy centres in the body originating from the Vedic system in India – there's a diagram included in the Resources section at the end), the seven main ones in the body are the root chakra, which is at the base of the spine; the sacral chakra, which is just near the belly button; the solar plexus chakra is in the middle of your body around where your stomach is; the heart chakra is at your heart; the throat chakra is at your throat; the third eye chakra is in between your eyebrows and the crown chakra is on the top of your head. I also connect to the Earth star chakra, which is below your feet in the ground and occasionally the soul star chakra, which is above your head. Each chakra also traditionally has different qualities and colours associated with it.

This chakra clearing continued on my forest walks for days. Each session felt like an energetic reset. I'd return home feeling lighter, clearer, more vibrant.

Then the energy started to shift and I began to receive, see, feel and simply become aware of different things happening in each of my chakras as I brought in the energy to clear them.

Each time it was something new.

I saw different coloured crystal formations in each of the chakras. I had beautiful flowers flourishing from each. Dragons cleared and anchored into each. One time each chakra was a different planet from our solar system, imbuing me with the qualities of the particular planet (for example, Mars was at my root chakra and it gave me fire and grounded power). Another time each showed me a different quality (this time the root became a heart-pumping valve bringing up the currents from the Earth, whilst the sacral chakra became a magnet to call in whatever it desires).

You get the picture. It was such a deeply magical experience, which literally changed me.

I also started sensing a cave begin to form at my Earth star chakra, beneath my feet in the ground. I began filling it with the energy of money, which turned into golden coins – abundant and overflowing. It was there for days and I felt like I had access to ancient vaults of wealth buried deep in the Earth.

It was around then that I had an idea to start sharing some of the chakra experiences I had been having. So I launched a programme on embodying your creative power and sold 60% of the spaces I wanted to fill before I even did a more public launch. Something was definitely beginning to shift. I could feel the power of the energetic experiences I had been receiving.

The next piece of clear guidance I received was to 'start writing in the waters.' I had an upcoming trip planned to the Indian Ocean so I gathered myself, ready to begin writing the book it wanted to be. The trip didn't quite turn out the way I thought, as not much writing happened.

But what *did* happen was a deeper attunement to the Earth's currents. Immersed in the elements, I found myself communing with the waters, feeling into how we describe and embody flow. Also how we use water analogies so often to describe money.

Something was coming closer. I could feel it. But it wasn't quite ready. I was still trying to *control* the process.

I eventually had to let this go, and it was then that I could feel the book quietly whispering to come 'deeper' to meet it.

To do that I needed let go of all the noise – anything that was distracting me, keeping me busy. So I began releasing things – I came off Facebook, left any groups I was a part of, stopped watching Netflix and YouTube, paused or cancelled all forms of digital input. I let it all go – so I could hear my own voice again. So I could meet the book on its terms, not mine.

Then it was time. In the container of a powerful, held energy session, I finally went down to the root of the book.

Beneath the Earth's layers, into a pool of liquid gold at the core and out into another dimension, is the only way to describe it. It felt like the all-ness and nothingness at the same time. The centre point of creation. Zero point. I spent some time there bathing in that space. Letting its aliveness vibrate in every single one of my cells.

Something shifted that day, and the words started flowing out of me. But they weren't all directly related to money.

I continued to connect to the book, which had now moved to the golden pool at the core of the Earth, and which became filled with DNA, to re-code and shift me. This is where I started to receive more stories, codes, words, activations, frequencies – all around power, love, being your full self. I was shown that all the currents on Earth originate from here and we have access to them. Everything is inter-connected, everything flows – in and out, like the seasons and cycles of Earth.

And then something wild and beautiful began to happen.

My chakras started rooting, not just within me, but across the Earth and Cosmos. Some grounded in sacred sites: Uluru, a pyramid deep in the Amazon under Peru, the temples of Egypt, into Atlantis beneath the ocean. Others anchored in far galaxies: Andromeda, Sirius.

My crown had to root into the liquid gold at the core of Gaia, where the book's energy firmly originated from. To receive Her codes, Her activation, as the golden energy passed down from the crown into every chakra – third eye, throat, heart, solar plexus, sacral and root. As this happened each chakra received the golden liquid which turned on the image of a symbol. A code.

And with each one, a younger version of me appeared. Each holding a piece of the truth I had forgotten. Each carrying gifts I had once known. I share more about them in the book.

It's then that I started to accept, to *know*, that it was a book about more than just money. I started to see the perfection and beauty in the entire journey I had been on with the book. It had been reminding and guiding me back into my power, which is rooted in the currents of the Earth and my body.

I started to see how the journey I had been taken on linked so closely to the elements. The alchemical paintings I was doing were like fire. (I also like to see the aligned action that began to happen towards the end of the experience also being fire.) The yin yoga experience grounding more into my body was the Earth. The magical chakra walks resembled the air. And the guidance to start writing in the waters deepening into its connection with money, of course linked to water.

All elements. All part of the whole.

I could see how the work I had been doing in my business with leaders, alongside writing the book, was also intricately connected. I even soft launched a 1:1 programme called Embodied Power in 2023 right before I committed to writing this book (then known to me as *Embodied Money*). But it didn't quite feel like the right time so I let it go. But now I can see, I was already receiving it.

When I looked back at my journals from the last few years, I realised: I had been writing about embodied love. About embodied power. About embodied magic. About being an embodied leader.

Over and over again. It was all connected.

And all of it: every step, every vision, every activation, fed the book you are about to read.

LET'S BEGIN

I thought that this book you are reading was going to be a book solely about money. I'd been journeying with the spirit of the book (which was titled *Embodied Money*), connecting to it, following its guidance as we co-created together for 20 months. I was hoping it would all come together in this perfect transmission that would be a *new* way to connect with money, live with money, be with money, receive money and ultimately embody money.

Reading back over the many journals I kept, and recalling moments where I could hear the quiet whispers of other book titles coming to me (which I chose to ignore at the time), I see now how I was actually deepening into my power. Embodying more of who I am – my gifts, my unique way of seeing and showing up in the world, my way of leading.

Money is a part of it. Of course it is – it's a tool to make things happen in this world. And I did deepen my relationship with it (at the time, I described it like a teenage romance: intense, confusing, on-again, off-again). I'll share more in the Embodied Money section, because money is an essential current of power. But what I found goes far beyond that.

This is what happens when you co-create with Spirit. It is equally about the becoming, through the journey it takes you on, one step after the other. (If you are interested in this journey and how I co-created with the book, take a look at the Preface section).

I have unlocked the codes to my power, which include the deep wisdom of my body, my power to create, alchemise and make magic happen. It's a power rooted in the wisdom of the Earth and Cosmos. It's a power that I know I've always had. It's a power you have too, when you own who you are.

This is what I am sharing with you here. The pillars of what I believe contribute to power. The kind that lives within you, waiting to be remembered and embodied. It's a power here to support you to lead in the way only you can.

We live in a time when billionaires think they can rule the world and take what they want, focusing only on their own desires and profits. The patriarchy has placed way too much power in the strength of a few, and perpetuated the cycle of many not believing they have any power at all to change things. It values more masculine traits such as doing, striving, taking action. Traits like intuition, care, creativity and magic have been dismissed or seen as lesser. It is time to change this, but to do so you need to recognise *your* power to change things from the inside out. It's time to reclaim all of you.

You have a role to play, whether you're leading a global organisation, writing a book, teaching children, creating art, or simply claiming your own life. You are a leader. Your power matters.

This book is your invitation to embody that power and lead in the way only you can. You are here to bring your quirks, your magic, your gifts into the world.

Are you ready?

It begins by looking at power, laying the foundation for what your power is, and what it can become. I see power as its own energy but also made up of different facets, as it is a holistic, living force that contributes to your leadership.

Then the book moves through four elemental sections, as ultimately this is a book about alignment and flow, rooted in the wisdom of the Earth.

EARTH: EMBODIED LOVE

It starts with love. Love for yourself, love for others, love for this planet. Love lays the foundation for the power to believe in yourself;

the belief that you can make a difference. When your power is rooted in love, it becomes a frequency that heals and ignites. It softens defences, disarms fear, and invites others into their own liberation.

Embodied Love is the code that will unlock the roots of your power.

WATER: EMBODIED MONEY

Money is integral to power. It is here to support you to embody more of your power, and to co-create with you. It is a tool for deeper impact.

This section invites you to look at your relationship with money, alongside the frequency and spirit of money, so that you can become partners, and welcome in money's support as you embody your power. Simultaneously, as you begin to embody your power you open to the resources that want to flow toward you, as a natural response to your embodied truth.

Embodied Money unlocks the codes to more flow, alignment and abundance.

AIR: EMBODIED MAGIC

You are a deeply powerful creator and it's time to let your intuition, your knowing, your alchemy be an integral part of your leadership. When you own your creative, spiritual and energetic gifts unapologetically, you stop leaking energy trying to explain, justify or hide these parts of you away.

This section includes spells, tools and activations of alchemy, magic and creation. Embodied Magic IS a reminder of the codes and creative power you were born with.

FIRE: EMBODIED LEADER

Lastly, I invite you to step into the leader you *really* are. A leader who chooses themselves fully and doesn't wait to be chosen. A leader who is rooted in love and their unique flavour and essence, because this is the only way for it to feel authentic. A leader who *knows* who they are.

As mentioned, what form this takes is not important. What is, is that you feel it. Become it. Claim it. This section includes a number of tools, prompts and activating pieces here to support you. Embodied Leader is your call to embody the leadership only you can.

I invite you to take a look at the Contents page to get a feel for what is in here. (There is a lot, and it's not meant to be used in one go.)

After that, see what calls to you, where you are drawn to. Take a piece that resonates in your body (you'll feel it) and sit with it, explore it, use it like a spell, make it your own. This is how you will move forward embodying the codes of YOUR power. When you truly claim your power as a conscious co-creator in your own life, you get to choose who you are, what you do, who you be, and what works for you.

You could also use it like an oracle deck or bibliomancy tool, opening it to a random page and letting where you land guide you.

(Just to add, there are things included in each section which overlap into others, so take the information and use it wherever it best applies to you.)

At the end you can find some additional resources and ways to go further with my support, if it's calling you.

I hope this book reminds you of just how damn powerful you are and that your power is so, so welcome.

Lastly, I would like to acknowledge that as an able-bodied, educated, English-speaking, straight, cisgender woman, my experiences and viewpoints are rooted in these privileges. I also acknowledge that as a woman of colour, there are systemic barriers and biases I have faced (and continue to navigate) that shape my lived experience in ways others may not fully see. I hold both the privilege I do have and the marginalisation I experience with deep awareness. I recognise the unearned power that comes with certain aspects of my identity, and I honour those whose experiences differ from mine. Please know I will make mistakes, but I am doing my best to learn, grow and be a better ally to those who don't have the same.

I am so grateful to you for picking up this book. It is a great privilege to share some of my experiences and magic with you.

Here's to you being fully YOU in the world.

Much love

Tara

FOR THE ONES WHO'VE NEVER *REALLY* FIT IN

You've always seen things differently.

Even in rooms full of smart, capable people, you've often felt like you were holding something no one else could quite name.

Not better. Just... other.
Deeper. Wider. Beyond the constructs.

Maybe you've learned to translate your vision into more digestible language.
Maybe you've stayed quiet at times, waiting for the space where your full truth could land.
Or maybe you've kept going, knowing you were here to shape something that doesn't yet exist.

You are not too much.
You're not naive.
You ARE a visionary.

You see patterns others miss.
You feel into futures before they're tangible.
You hold a frequency that can challenge what's safe and familiar for others.

And while that's powerful, it can also feel isolating.

Where do you go when you're the one holding the bigger picture?
Who do you turn to when your ideas are met with silence, doubt, or subtle resistance?

How do you stay anchored when the path ahead doesn't look like anyone else's?

Your difference is not your weakness. It's your design.
The world doesn't need more conformity. It needs more courage. More clarity. More leaders who are willing to be seen in their wholeness.

If you've never quite fit in, maybe it's because you're here to lead what hasn't been created yet.

To bring through something that only *you* can carry.
To find (or create) the space where you don't have to translate, shrink, or explain.
To let yourself lead from your depth, truth and creative power.
To fully embody *your* frequency!

THE GOLDEN POOL

There was a time when the Gods, the Goddesses and dragons roamed the Earth. They lavished in the waters, soaking up their nourishment, soothing their bodies. They ate succulent fruits, bursting from the bushes. They lived in harmony with the animals as friends, companions on their journey.

They each knew their powers. Their strengths, their gifts. They had unique pieces that added to the whole.

One could call in love, create love, bring love to any situation.
Another embodied their humour – creating joy, laughter and fun in their wake.
There was a God of play and mischievousness, but all in good faith.

They knew that these gifts brought harmony to one another; it supported them to live in peace, in co-creation with one another.

Much time was spent valuing the land, each other and simply being.

They knew what a gift it was to simply be here, on Earth. To receive Her bounty, Her magic, Her holding.

They knew She carried great powers at Her core. A pool of liquid gold that could replenish them if they ever needed. It was the source of all their magic, the gifts that they held. They knew that they must live in communion with Earth and one another – for this to continue.

So they supported one another. Lent others their gifts. Looked out for each other.

Until one God came along, and wanted it all. This God didn't want to share. They wanted all the power of the golden pool – the codes it carried.

They tried to contain it, soak it all up so others couldn't get to it. But Gaia (Earth) knew this was happening and She decided to banish them all. She called the dragons to come and protect the golden pool; She built layers upon it, so it couldn't be found. Only the dragons could come in and out – becoming messengers and carriers of Her codes. They are still there protecting it.

Gaia reminds you of Her power – and that nobody can come close to the pool, for want of stealing its powers for themselves – She rages through hurricanes, tornadoes, volcanoes, earthquakes.

But the dragons still deliver the codes of the golden pool, to those ready for them.

This was a visualisation I received close to when this book was coming into form. It felt important to include it as the pool itself and the dragons became my connection to the book as it took shape.

THE DRAGONS

At the centre of the Earth, is a golden pool. It is pure, Divine Source energy. It is liquid power.

Its keepers are the dragons.

The dragons travel within the currents that come out of the golden pool.
They connect us to the source of all life.
The currents which move through Mother Earth: water, air and fire.
Her currents of creation.
They carry these energies and codes of life.

The dragons are here to call you back to this truth.
They are here to clear, burn away and transmute.
They are here to remind you of your power.
They are here to remind you that your power can change the world.

MESSAGES FROM THE ELEMENTAL POWER DRAGONS

EARTH DRAGON WISDOM

Your body is your power.
Your power is your body.
It is your lived, breathed and felt experience.
How you receive the world.
How you feel your way through.
How you experience the nuances.
Let your body guide you.
Let your body lead.
This is where you'll find your true power.

WATER DRAGON WISDOM

Nowhere to go.
Nothing to do.
Nowhere to be.
Formless.
Floating.
Flowing.
It can be what you will.
It can become what you want.
It wants to show you it can.

AIR DRAGON WISDOM

Like sparkles glistening under a midnight sun.
Effervescent footprints left by the unseen.
There's magic all around you.
It whispers in the wind.
It bellows in the thunder.
It comes to all who call its name.
Casts a spell for those who want to see.

FIRE DRAGON WISDOM

A glowing ember ignites.
Flame becomes fire.
Fierce, majestic strength.
It dissipates.
Then again burns bright.
It wants to play.
It wants to create.
As it warms the seeds of your becoming.

Embodied Power

We begin by looking at power: opening to the power that is already inside of you. Welcoming it in and either beginning, or deepening, your relationship with your unique power. The power I believe you are here to embody more fully as a leader. Remember this is a journey, I don't believe we ever get 'there' – wherever that elusive 'there' is.

This introduction section includes stories, activations and tools to lay the foundation for this. They are in no particular order, but are here to be used, dipped into and embodied, however you feel called to them.

FEELING POWER-LESS

A turquoise-tinged 1p (UK currency) coin rolled under the table. I quickly stomped on it to stop it disappearing into the black hole underneath the couch.

Placing it onto the table alongside the rest of the coppers and coins I'd scraped out of my purse. It didn't take long to count: £1.25. That is all I had to my name. £1.25.

Oh and over £30,000 worth of debt and loans.

How the fuck had it got to this?

It was December 2012 and I'd been staying at a friend's North London flat for the past six months, since quitting my job for the second time in 18 months. In those six months I'd been completely unemployed, maxing out my credit cards, while scouring job sites for work as a PA or office manager. Areas I really didn't want to work in again. I so badly wanted to start my own business – the problem was I didn't know what I wanted it to be in.

Why wasn't I able to make it work, in a system that so many others seemed to thrive in? It was easy enough: get up, go to work, get promoted, take holidays, buy a house, get married and have kids. The 'normal' way.

The thing is, there was something inside me that literally couldn't make myself do it. I found it soul-destroying, heart-crushing; and a part of me deep down inside knew I wasn't meant for that way. It wouldn't let me take another step forward in a full-time job, so I *had* to find another way.

This was the catalyst for what became the year (2013) I now look back on as my rock bottom, but also the year that set something alight inside of me, that fuelled the person I am today.

But at that moment I felt so completely and utterly powerless. I was broke and in a mountain of debt; desperately single; overflowing with self-loathing as I was still drinking regularly to excess to simultaneously numb and feel at the same time; and jobless, directionless, purposeless.

From here on I spiralled even deeper. I started dabbling in MDMA and Ecstasy – the party drugs that the friend I was staying with was into, although I had previously outright refused. I began doing them similarly to why I drank alcohol – to feel the expansive-loving-openness they gave me (as is the reason many people do them). I also found I could talk about things to the depth I wanted to. I could be *too* much; I could be me – fully, unashamedly, and it wasn't considered weird.

But the repercussion they had on my insanely sensitive system quickly began to create a new baseline for me that meant I felt super low all the time and anxiety became my new normal. This just sparked a desire to do more drugs, and to try and numb the feelings in any other way possible.

So began my brief foray into the online dating world. I vaguely remember Tinder hadn't quite gotten its wings at this point, but Plenty of Fish and OK Cupid were free and where it was at.

The whole experience, thankfully, lasted less than six months. My first actual date was with a guy who invited me to see a metal band, with a coffee beforehand. I wasn't a big music person, unless it was cheesy rock or pop stuff, but wanting to please – and go on a date – I agreed to it. It was there that I learned that the guy had just been released from prison on parole, also had no money and no job, and I had to pay for the pre-gig drink with what little money I had. I'm all for giving people a chance and have no problems paying, but this didn't feel good at all. I made my excuses and skipped the band.

After that it was purely guys messaging me interested in *one* thing only. I'm not an idiot and get that this is more than likely the case with many people on there... but I wanted to be in a relationship, a partnership. This is the part where I look back and feel sad for younger me. I went along with it. Not at first, but it quickly crept up on me, and I found myself agreeing to do things the guys wanted, having one-night stands, even though I didn't really want to. Hoping that maybe, just maybe, one would end up as my happily ever after. Of course they didn't. It actually resulted in me feeling lower in myself than before it had all begun!

(Please know I have absolutely no issue with one-night stands, or anything else between consenting adults. I just did it from a place rooted in low self-worth.)

I share this experience as it shows just how powerless I felt at that time. How intricately connected my sense of power was to my financial situation, my ability to look after myself, and have a purpose in the world. As well as, of course, what I would do for others and how badly I wanted to be accepted and loved to feel worthy.

I look back on this pivotal low point and all I really wanted was to be rescued by a knight in shining armour. But things didn't unfold that way for me. I had to find my power within and do what I could to change my situation. I had to pick myself up and begin again. Taking one step after the next, holding on to the whisper of faith I had deep down inside that I could turn things around.

I knew the one thing I could do to change things was to start to look after my health. So I did.

I started to let go of the drinking; the over-eating of comfort foods that made me feel bloated and sluggish. I started to practice yoga a few times a week. This changed everything and became the foundation for who I am today. I began a new relationship with my body – I got to know my body for me. I began to actually like myself.

This then lead to me joining a free life coaching training event I happened to come across, which opened the doors to me being able to re-train as a health coach.

I began my business there and it evolved into something, which I totally made up! I get to do all the things I love, such as colour and chakra activations, healing deep-dives, painting, writing and more. Above all I began to remember the power I had inside to choose, and to change my life. I began to remember the deeply powerful, creative little girl I knew was still inside of me.

(I share a lot more of this journey in my other books, which you can find details for in the Resources section at the end.)

I look at where I am today and my life is vastly different. I am a different person. It's through taking one step after the other to come back to myself. Trusting the process and unfolding. Letting it be cyclical. Letting myself mess up again and again. Remembering my power to create. My power to alchemise. Leaning into the holding, love and support from the physical (guides, mentors, healers, friends, family and more) and non-physical, which includes creating a new supportive relationship with money. Learning, realising and knowing in my bones that I am here to create and lead new ways, and support others to do so.

In this book, I share more examples from my journey alongside the tools, codes, spells, magic and activations that I use myself and share with clients.

I believe that if you have been drawn to this book, you are a magical, unique and magnificent leader, here to vision and create a new world. It starts with remembering, choosing and claiming your power.

BECOME WHO YOU CAME HERE TO BE

Your soul chose to incarnate at this time.
At a time when the world is going through massive upheaval, change and disruption.
At a time where things are crumbling, breaking, falling apart.
At a time when leaders from all corners of the planet are needed to create change rooted in love, care and compassion for all.

Your soul chose to be here.
To create hope, new ways of be-ing, do-ing, thinking, living.
To create in the way that only it can.
To create in its fullest expression.

To be this, to do this.
It is time to embody your wholeness.
It is time to embody your fullness.
It is time to embody your power.

EMBODIED POWER

Embodied Power is choosing to go ALL in on the life you came to Earth for.

It's remembering, unlocking, and embodying the codes of your unique power.

It's aligning with the power of the Earth as a Divine being – Gaia; Her currents of creation and life force energy, and the elements through which they flow: Earth, water, air and fire (plus Spirit). It's recognising you are a part of Gaia and as such also have access to this power to create.

It's burning away the patterns and addictions that keep you playing small and self-sabotaging. It's healing ancestral, past-life and childhood traumas and patterns; knowing it's now time to receive the gifts from the richness of your past.

It's tapping into the deep wisdom of your body, letting it be your guide. Letting it be your co-creator and your partner as you embody your power.

It's committing to a life where you are present on Earth and will do what it takes to look after your whole self, others and the Earth, as we are all connected.

It's doing whatever it takes to be a co-creator in your life whilst also deeply leaning into the support available to you (seen and unseen) and guidance from your intuition. It's remembering you are magical, Divine, and have limitless power and support available to you.

It's knowing in your bones that you are here to dismantle, disrupt, re-write and create the new, in the way only you can do.

It's recognising you are a leader and it is now time to step into this, to own this, embody this and live it fully. Unapologetically, unashamedly, boldly.

It is time.

THE POWER OF YOU

There's a part inside of you that knows your power.

It's a power that can create miracles.
It's a power that can change the world.

It's the power you bring, by being FULLY you.

RE-WRITING POWER

When you hear the word 'power', what do you instantly think of?

I'm guessing leaders of countries or organisations, someone with lots of money, body-builders, strength or endurance athletes, perhaps your old headteacher in school or someone that influenced you in some way, or maybe a moment when you did something you were proud of.

Power can mean lots of things, but in more recent times it has found its home in the strength area (because of the patriarchal system of values) – often being attributed to someone who has control or dominance over another or others.

As power actually means having the ability to influence, this often comes down to money, to having deep pockets, which can buy their way. It's also about having the confidence to do something or act in a particular way, and it's like we're literally trained not to do that from the moment we are born and have systems and constructs laid out for us. In fact many of us have learned that our power is un-safe and not something we can trust, let alone bring out into the world.

This is putting it super simply, as I don't want to linger any longer in what power *has* been.

Ultimately this book is about creating the new. Re-writing, or even remembering that power is so much more than this. Power is available to us all, not just those in positions of authority, or those with money (there's no denying these things help, and I go into this more in the Embodied Money section).

But, the way I see it, true power comes from deep within and is a part of what makes you, you.

This is your invitation, your activation to come home to it now. Your power is needed now more than ever.

THIS IS WHAT POWER IS TO ME…

Power is trusting myself.
Power is saying no.
Power is resting.
Power is listening to my body.
Power is knowing what I like and don't like.
Power is knowing I am enough.
Power is doing things my way.
Power is softness.
Power is magnetism.
Power is pleasure.
Power is letting it be messy.
Power is not caring what others think.
Power is getting it 'wrong'.
Power is making mistakes.
Power is compassion for others.
Power is caring about the whole.
Power is being my full self.

What is power to you?

WELCOMING YOUR POWER

For many I find your power can be seen as an un-integrated essence or energy within you, as often it's a part that you've had to disown, shut down, bury or even banish. As a child, if your power came out in an 'unacceptable' way such as anger, you might have got in trouble and learned it wasn't welcome. If your power is softer, gentler and more inward, you might have been bullied or shut down by someone else whose power was stronger. So you hid it away, ashamed of what was yours.

Just to be clear, I don't feel power is one thing for each of us. I believe we all have different facets, threads, faces to our power, each contributing to our overall power. I see power as an embodying of all of it – a welcoming of your wholeness.

But, it's time to get to know what this is. To open the door to what this could be, with an openness and knowing that it will change, evolve and grow.

A couple of ways you can re-claim your relationship with your power, and what it feels and looks like right now, is to connect with it through a visualisation, or simply journal with it.

Bring your attention inward and invite your power in. Get to know it as an energy – what it feels, looks, and/or sounds like. Start to experience it from this perspective. Get to know its qualities and deepen your relationship with it like you would a new friend.

When I've guided clients to connect with their power they've had a mix of experiences from feeling their power as pure joy; or a soft, expansive, loving energy; to wild, sacred rage that is fiercely protective.

My own power showed itself to me as a peacock, when I first started tuning into it! I didn't like this at first as I often felt peacocks had an over the top, too-much vibe! But then I fell in love with it, and I took it as a metaphor for being proud of my unique-ness, for showing off who I am unapologetically. To let my power be that loud, bold, ME.

There is no right or wrong way for your power to be. And as mentioned above it is very likely more than one thing, that will change and evolve over time.

If you want to explore this further, I have a number of visualisations which guide you to connect to your power on my Insight Timer channel, as well as resources in my web shop. Details for both are in the Resources section at the end.

THE POWER IN BE-ING IN A BODY

Stop.
Slow down.
Take a moment to simply be.
Alone with your body.
Where you won't be disturbed.

Become present in your body.
Start to consciously breathe into it.
Notice any sensations, how it's feeling.
Just be present.
Breathing into your body.
Simply be-ing with yourself.
Without judgement or expectation.

As you sit with your body.
Perhaps ask it to show you pleasure.
See what you notice, what you feel.
Let yourself experience it.
Be with it.
Hold it.

Then you could ask your body to show you play.
See what comes up this time.
Receive it.
Be with it.
Don't move on yet.
Keep holding it.

Now you could ask your body to show you power.
Feel this.
Let your body show you your power.
Where it comes from.
Receive it. Experience it.
Get to know it.
Does it have anything it wants to share with you?

Exploring different things/feelings/emotions/ways of being that you want to experience, by asking your body to guide you, is quite a profound experience. If you don't feel anything the first, or even few times trying this, don't be hard on yourself or think it's not working. Most people are so disconnected from their bodies it's hard to notice the sensations as they are often very subtle to begin.

FEAR OF YOUR OWN POWER

There's a part inside of you (maybe a few) that fears the power you embody.
That fears what you are capable of.
Fears what might happen to others.
Fears what might happen if you turned up the dial.

The part inside likely fears you won't have control.
That if you open the lid it will be un-wielding, raging, rampant, destructive.
It will be like a feral, wild animal let loose after a lifetime of caging.
There will be no saying what *might* happen.

You might be banished.
You might be judged.
You'll hurt others.
You'll create chaos.

All the bad things that *could* happen, if you open up to your power.

But, what if... what if... none of that is true?!

What if you open to a power that has your back; cares deeply for you and others; creates magic and miracles; supports your dreams; champions your mission; co-creates your vision for yourself and the world.

Maybe it's time to stop fearing what could happen, stop fearing the worst. Remember, you are a heart-rooted, caring, compassionate being, and any power that comes from you will always be based in this.

Take a moment to connect to those parts inside. The younger version or versions of you still holding the power reins, and let them know it's okay. Things have changed. You have got this. It's time to take over, and let your power out.

GIVING AWAY YOUR POWER

Where is it time to bring awareness, love, compassion and releasing, when it comes to giving your power away? We are literally trained to give away our power from the moment we are born. Our power of choice gets muted by the fact that we are born into a system with rules and obligations that we *have* to follow.

So without getting too heady and judgemental about it all – it's simply to bring awareness, so it can start to release: where do you still give your power away?

Here are some of my bigger ones: some are gone, some I'm still working with…

- Addictions – eating, watching endless series on Netflix or YouTube, and previously drinking alcohol.
- Believing I have no choice – that I have to do what's right, best, or good, and I don't get to put my needs first.
- Compartmentalising who I am to fit in – this happened often when I felt I couldn't talk about the spiritual things I am interested in, and what and how I live, work and be in the world. It's a bit like a hangover from the 'old' me and life I had, working in regular jobs and doing things as I was taught to, to belong.
- Not taking responsibility for myself – this is a layered one and comes from not really committing to be on Earth. I think a part of me also never fully trusted that I could provide for myself. I also used to say a lot that *life is short*, so let's just enjoy it (I do believe this, but these days I think further ahead, because I actually want to be here fully).

- Putting others first and doing everything I could to accommodate for them. Whilst I did this in friendships a bit, I certainly used to do it in romantic relationships. I would completely ditch myself and my needs to please a guy and cater to his needs, as I thought it meant he'd want me more.
- Not setting boundaries – this is a common one, and definitely links to putting others first, wanting to please and be liked.
- Not claiming my magic – this is something I'll be going into more in the book, and I know I'm not alone here. We've been taught not to trust our magic, our intuition, our ways of seeing and receiving that go beyond the logical, which leads into the next point.
- Trusting others' opinions over my own – even if I *felt* something or *knew* something in my bones; if someone else had a different way or opinion I'd listen to that over myself. This one rarely happens anymore (except occasionally if I'm tired I might discount my own perspective).

WHERE DO YOU GIVE YOUR POWER AWAY?

- To people, places, habits, distractions, beliefs, stories, patterns and more?
- How much time and energy have you given to this?
- What parts of yourself have you dulled, muted, diluted or forgotten through this?

I TRUST MY POWER

I trust my power

I trust my power

I trust my power

I trust my power

I trust my power

I trust my power

I trust my power

I trust my power

I trust my power

THE POWER IN RAGE

Maybe it's the peri-menopausal years no longer letting me take any BS. Perhaps it's all the anger, betrayal, times I've conformed, people who've infuriated me with their sheer disregard for the planet or other people, things I've stuffed down – now making themselves known. Things I was picking up on or carrying that weren't even mine. Either way, I went through a period of rage!

Sheer. Fucking. Pure. Raw. Rage.

It needed to breathe.
It needed to be heard.
It needed to be acknowledged.

I let it. I felt it. I painted it. I screamed it until I was raw. I moved it. I un-caged it.

I welcome my rage. It is fuel for my creative power. It's life force energy here to make things happen.

There is power in rage.

As I was getting close to completing this book, I had my first negative rating and review on Insight Timer (a pivotal moment I knew would come at some point!). And interestingly it was on my 'Embody your power' visualisation. Basically anger had arisen for the person listening when they'd connected to their power; it hadn't felt good and the person didn't want this to be a part of their power.

Of course I don't know the specifics, but it was such a powerful reminder and confirmation of how we try to bypass the things that don't feel so good, and that power IS made up of more than just things like strength, courage, fierce-ness. There's soooo much power in anger, which is often unresolved. I invite you to (with support and holding if you need it) let your anger, your rage, be there. Get to know it, speak to it, express it. It also needs space to breathe. More often than not once it has had this space, it will be a catalyst for an even more magical power that's bubbling beneath the surface. Also, sometimes we simply need anger and rage to get shit done, to make changes, to be a driving force!

I'VE ALWAYS KNOWN THIS...

I'm not here to follow the rules laid out for me.
The conditioned masculine way of doing business.
Or even the pseudo-feminine way, which to me feels like a watered down way to simply make it in a man's world.

I'm not here to follow a circadian rhythm. Or even a week with 5 days on and 2 off.
My inner cycle, which follows its own schedule, IS my power. I *know* that when I let it guide me I have endless days for be-ing and can get (aligned) stuff done in an instant.

I'm not here to listen to advice from those that don't know what it's like to live in my body: to feel so, so much; to keep pushing, forcing, and to focus on profit only!

I've so often got pulled back into the trap of comparison-itis.
Feeling not enough. Like someone else knows better.
If I just do it *that* way maybe it'll get easier; maybe I'll find the elusive answer that society and conditioning has had me searching for, for as long as I can remember, because without it – I'm not enough!

I have yo-yo'd between deeply trusting myself and my guidance, then thinking I'm not enough. I should get help from someone who is.

NO MORE.

It is time to stop comparing, thinking I'm doing it wrong.
It's time to stop searching outside of myself.

From this moment forward I am fully leaning into doing it my way. It's a way that I can only uncover by deeply listening within. Nobody can give me the answer or discern the way but me.

I've always known this.

Now it's time to go ALL in.

Are you with me?

YOU GET TO DO THIS

Something a few of my mentors have reminded me of in different contexts – is the powerful reminder and knowing that you GET to do this. You GET to create something, lead in the way only you can, and affect others. You GET to be who you want to be, make choices, change your life, do what it takes to be your full self…

It's so easy to fall into victim mode when things feel hard – I certainly have! But as I've been reminded, and now deeply feel, is the sheer privilege that I GET to be who I am and do what I do. I GET to pursue my heart, my magic, my creativity. The majority of humans on this planet don't get this opportunity and just having a job with money coming in to survive is the only focus.

Also of course it's okay to be human and feel the difficult times. But I'm guessing if you are here reading this that you do have opportunities, privileges and more power than many. So remember you GET to do this. There is power in this remembering.

YOUR POWER IS MEDICINE

Not just for you, but for the world.

Your gifts, your intuition, your creative fire, your ability to give form to the formless, were never meant to stay hidden in the shadows. They were born to breathe, to move, to heal, to awaken.

Your power does not threaten.
It liberates.
It does not compete.
It creates space.

When you stand unapologetically in your truth, you don't just shine, you ignite something ancient and alive in others.

When you trust the brilliance that moves through you, you become a living invitation – calling in those who've been quietly searching for exactly what you hold.

When you embody your power – not as performance, but as presence – the world shifts.

The right clients find you.
The aligned opportunities arrive.
The creations that have been waiting on your 'yes' begin to flow.

This is the work.
This is the gift.

This is the medicine.

And it begins with you.

THE CODES YOU CARRY

You carry the codes of all that you are here for.
They are infused with the wisdom of the ages.
The knowing of your lineage.
The miracle of life.

These codes are not for anyone else.
They are yours to unlock.
They are yours to receive.
To step into.
To become.

The codes of your calling. Your gifts. Your talents.
They are not by accident.
They are not by mistake.
They simply are.

They are yours.
Will you claim them?

Earth: Embodied Love

This section lays the foundation for your power. It is only through love that we can change the world for the good of all. This starts with being here on Earth fully. Loving yourself, choosing yourself, nourishing yourself, holding and supporting yourself, receiving love from others – from community, and from here bringing this love into the world.

I see Embodied Love as a return to your wholeness, to yourSELF.

There are codes, stories, activations, tools and guidance to remind you of this. I invite you to dip in and out as you need.

BE-ING ON EARTH

Being on Earth can feel so hard, too much, at times. Especially if you are open and sensitive to everything. To the way things are – the overwhelming lack of empathy, care and compassion. If trauma has affected you (and it has all of us), you may find it easier to not be fully in your body. Human-ing is hard!

It's so easy to not feel safe to be fully you – maybe you won't be accepted, maybe you have real and cellular memories of danger from being fully you. It's so tempting to want to escape, jump in and out of your body, numb, avoid, create a bubble where you don't have to engage or be fully in the world.

But that isn't the way forward. Of course there will be times when you need a cocoon of replenishment and respite, but it's also about navigating the world, starting to do what you can to feel safe, held, protected on Earth.

To create change, to have experiences, to live on Earth, you need to be fully present. Let the energies, feelings and sensations move through your body. Feel it, be with it all; the body can be a powerful transmuter and alchemiser. It can even alchemise the experiences into gold – ideas, a current, creations, all you desire.

But first it must be felt, lived, experienced.

THE EARTH IS CREATIVE POWER

Everything you create comes from the Earth.
Your body. Your energy. Your ideas. Your resources.

Gaia is not just ground beneath your feet, She is a galactic, sentient being. A living intelligence. The original creative force you are part of.

When you deepen your relationship with the Earth, through your root chakra, through your Earth star chakra, through your body, you reconnect to the source of all creation.

This is not separate from your power. It *is* your power.

When you are anchored here, you become stable, grounded, replenished.
Creation flows more freely.
Ideas become embodied.
Desire becomes form.

Your creativity, your business, your leadership, it all starts here.
Held by the Earth. Powered by the Earth. In relationship with the Earth.
This is the foundation.

COMMIT TO BEING ON EARTH

I call all parts of me back – the parts that left when life got difficult, painful and messy. I call all of myself back together now.

I declare my commitment to being fully here on Earth in my body. I commit to my life in the fullest. To being and bringing all of myself. To deeply accepting and loving all of me.

I commit to being here on Earth through it all – the good, the messy, the incredible, the exhilarating, the painful – all of it, as a part of what it means to be human.

I commit to holding and being with the parts of me that are scared, tentative and nervous about this.

I vow to do what it takes always to deeply support myself always, as I live a life fully present, here on Earth.

This is the only way forward. I commit to being here for it all.

AN ODE TO MY BODY

We've had a complicated history.
I felt you were a curse.
I tried to silence your signals.
Avoid you.
Mould you.
Do anything to shape you.
To make you fit in.

But you were never going to.
You were always different.
Deeply feeling.
Unapologetically sensitive.
Wildly magical.
Always you.

I wish I'd known then what a gift you are.
How you've held me unconditionally.
Recovered again and again.
With grace I didn't earn,
But was given freely.

You've led me quietly.
Shaped how I show up.
Guided my creative fire.
Been a portal to my magic.
A trusted business confidante.
A keeper of my wisdom.

I now delight in your unique needs.
I give thanks that you pick things up so fast.
That you always seem to 'know'.

Your deeply feeling, loving embrace is my happy place.
I'm so grateful I get to call you home.

PUT IT ALL DOWN FOR A MOMENT

It is so tiring trying to be something you aren't. Wearing masks, identities, roles that have been assigned to you. It is bone-bloody-deep tiring.

Let it go. Just for a moment. Imagine it all peeling off you, falling down, down, down, on to the Earth.

Take a breath. Let your shoulders drop.

Feel the recalibration, as your body remembers this.

The stillness, the peace, beginning to take over.

Sit here for a moment.

Return to you. Simply, powerfully you. Just as you are.

Let yourself drop deeper into it. Like you're floating down into a womb cave within the heart of the Earth.

Let your heart melt into this. Let your body be cocooned here. Held deeply. Closely.

Take a moment to replenish, to fill up.

To remember... this is home.

You can find a visualisation called 'A moment of replenishment' guiding you into this on my free Insight Timer channel. Details are in the Resources section at the end.

LET IT BE MESSY

You've likely been holding it together your whole life. Keeping the calm, avoiding conflict. Stuffing down emotions that stray from the 'acceptable' list. When big life events happened only the positive was shared. The hard times got brushed under the rug, to be dealt with in therapy – or in most cases, never at all.

Sometimes there's so much 'stuff' still swimming about within, layers under the layers, it can be hard to stop. To even let go for a moment. For fear a cavern of darkness might come spilling out. Pandora's proverbial box will open.

So you continue on. It's business as usual. Or is it? It gets harder and harder to carry on.

Unless you let all the stuff out, you won't make a change.

When you feel held and supported, deeply, at your core. You are safe to be messy. To let go fully.

I invite you to deeply lean into the messiness of it all – it's going to be a constant in these times we live in. You have to learn to let it be messy and show up anyway.

A MOMENT OF PAUSE

There's so much depth, beauty and wisdom inside of you.
Be with it.
Deeply breathe into this truth... this knowing.
In the stillness.
Be held by it, nurtured by it, soothed by it.
Sink even deeper, down, down, down.
Into the place between worlds,
Where your soul's shadow resides.
Let it be a resting place for a while.

BEING HELD

Imagine feeling so held from beneath, from your root, that you can fully let go.
You feel yourself softening, even in the smallest places in your body (your jaw, between your eyebrows, your lips) where you didn't realise you were holding on.
As you surrender, your body drops deeply into stillness.
It's like landing inside a cocoon of pure peace, like being held in the quiet depths of the ocean.

Here you can hear yourself.
Here you can simply be.
Nothing to hold. Nothing to do. Nothing to remember.
Control becomes a distant concept, dissolving into nothingness.
All that remains is you, stripped bare, naked in your vulnerability, and that is enough.

You feel your connection to everything and nothing.
This is the place to sit in silence.
To remember your truth.
To let yourself be held.

From here you receive what you need: rest, recalibration, healing.
The release of layers and conditioning,
The weight of carrying it all.
Or it may be play and joy, a dance with life's current... pleasure, passion, a deepening of desire.

It is alignment with your deepest truth.
A meeting with energy that awakens your creative power.
A heart opening beyond all limits.
Every nuance, every shift, every possibility embodied.
This is the strength of remembering who you are at your core.

CLAIMING YOUR BODY SOVEREIGNTY

As someone who picks up energies like a wet sponge, I have to ground into the Earth, clear my energy regularly and even create a bubble of protection – if I feel like I am going to be immersed in a lot of other people's stuff.

In the past I've hesitated to use the word 'protection' as it feels like 'me versus others', and perpetuates much of the separation I already feel a lot of the time. But, I've found that if I'm in crazy traffic or a busy shopping centre (which rarely happens), I can come home a complete wreck, emotional, exhausted and feeling absolutely all over the place, if I don't create some sort of energetic protection for myself. These days I see it more like wearing oil on my skin – a soothing layer which supports me whilst also keeping things out that I don't need.

However, recently I was going through a LOT of body stuff. I'm talking a few months almost continuously of a sore throat, cold symptoms, then stomach issues, aches in my body – nothing was wrong with me on a medical level, and it felt completely overwhelming and honestly unnecessary. I know my body processes a lot and whenever I go through something, up-level, create something that stretches me, or simply shift into a new intention I feel e-v-e-r-y-t-h-i-n-g in my body. But this was non-stop and I was done!

I started to journal with my body, asking it what was going on. This is what came through...

'Dear body,

What is going on? Why are you going through so much right now? So much releasing, clearing, physical pain. This is getting exhausting. I feel depleted, low, sad, like I don't even want to be here anymore. What is going on? Please tell me.

I'm processing a lot right now. Collectively. Within the Earth. The Cosmos. Ancestrally. This lifetime. So many things moving through to be released.

Why do you have to do it for everyone? I am not here for that. I don't choose to take that on.

I thought that's what you wanted. To take away other people's pain. To prove your worth and value. To be a good girl. To feel useful, valid and of significance.

I don't anymore. If I ever did, I take that back now. I am NOT, I repeat, I am absolutely NOT here to process everyone else's shit. I send it back to each and every one/thing to deal with. I am here to thrive, flourish, be magical. NOT to process all the collective shit. Enough now. Do you get that? Give it all back please. Let it all go. Step into your goddamn sovereignty.

I want you to be my partner. My co-creator in all the magic we are now here to create. We've done so much healing of our own together, and if there is more, I am here for that, always. But just ours, okay? Other people can handle their own. We need to see them in their power, okay. Stop being a martyr, victim, people pleaser, saviour – all that shit. NO MORE.

I want us to start to feel all the possibility. The joy. The magic. The creative potential from feeling. This is the power you need to now begin feeling.

What do you need from me to support you?

Nourish and look after me immaculately. Impeccably. With so much love and tenderness.

It's time to let go of all the shit from everyone else. RIGHT NOW.

DONE. DONE. DONE.'

This conversation opened me to how I had still been taking on things for others and from that day on I claimed my body sovereignty, like a stake in the ground! From the next day all my body symptoms disappeared and I felt like I could feel my edges again. I now claim my body sovereignty daily, sometimes more. It feels more empowering than putting on protection, although I still do that sometimes too. It's like a beam of power coming up from the core of the Earth, into my core then radiating out from my body.

This is what I say, in case you want to borrow it or create your own from it:

'My body is sovereign; my body is mine. I am not here to process shit for anyone else. Their stuff is their own. I am only here to move through that which is here for me, to support me on my journey, for my highest good. Anything else is NOT welcome – (then I often swear as it feels activating and powerful) it can fuck off, fuck off, fuck off.'

Since the months of symptoms, it's been three months (as I am writing this) that I have not had one physical symptom that I couldn't attribute to something I knew I was personally processing. (I recognise we can also pick up bugs, and other physical symptoms from others, but I am speaking more of energetic symptoms that come from processing emotions etc.)

CHORDS OF RESONANCE

If something touches you, moves you, or strikes a chord.
There may be something in it for you.
Something to release, burn away, un-hook from, or delete.
Something to learn, carry forward and embody more deeply.

Let the chords of resonance in your body remember.
Pay attention to them.
Listen to them.
Honour them.
They will show you the way.

'DARK' POWERS

When I started coming even more out of hiding – sharing the parts of me (like my love for dragons and past lives) that I wouldn't have dreamed of before, with certain people and in certain places like LinkedIn, I began to feel a lot of contraction from a younger version of me.

She was stomping her foot down, folding her arms, not having any of it. I could feel her wall of 'no' between my heart and chest.

When I connected to her more deeply I learned pretty fast that it was five-year-old me, who *knew* her power. But, she also remembered the scarier things she could access being so fully open. She could feel dark energies, and knew that some people wanted to do her harm.

It brought back a particularly vivid memory of being captured in the kindergarten playground by a bunch of boys. I was then taken into a big play-rocket-ship, tied up and not allowed to leave. I did manage to escape, but this is a memory that has often haunted me as I remember being so, so scared. I know there are possible past life and galactic threads in it. But the thing that got me so freaked out was I really felt to my core that the 'leader', another child like myself, wanted to harm me. To this day I can recall that fear I felt.

I was of course told by the teachers to stop being silly, I was making it up, and to get back out there. Encouraging me not to trust myself, or what I felt. (So began the journey of trying to dull how much I felt, even just gradually.)

But, when I sat with little me, now as the adult I am – I reminded her I've got her now. I'm here to protect her. We also had a guardian angel as a child, and magical dragons that were always there. They still are, in fact they're back more strongly than ever, and they are here for us any time we need them.

Whilst my younger self loves dragons, they may not resonate with you. If your inner child needs and wants some extra protection, ask them what they would like.

OPENING UP TO A FULL SENSORY EXPERIENCE

Really feeling, hearing, experiencing everything is how I connect to the current of creation I feel from the Earth and galaxies. It's how I receive deep intuitive guidance that blows me away every time, it's so on point. It's how I feel so much, which makes me give a damn about humanity and our planet, and want to make a difference. It's what gives me inspiration to create beauty in this world. It's my edge in how I hold space for others' to access their gifts – to be themselves fully.

I began to numb and shut down my senses, in particular my hearing and how much my body feels, as a child. The death of my mother when I was eight and the resulting life circumstances were just too much for my highly sensitive self.

It's taken years to begin to open up to these senses and really let myself experience the world through them. Decades living in London, coupled with commuting, noises and busyness, has always felt overwhelming for me. So keeping my senses a little numb was my body's way of protecting me. Keeping me from experiencing and feeling so much. Too much.

As I've gone through my own healing journey I have shed layers with lots of support, which has allowed me to begin to do this. But it's only now as I prioritise my wellbeing, with daily walks in nature, and being present here on Earth – in my body, that these senses are really coming back online (so to speak).

They are also integral to my gifts and creativity.

At some point along the way you may have shut down to fit in. To not feel so much. To be anything but your full self.

But this is what is needed.

Where have you been numbing, avoiding or dulling your senses to not feel so much? What could you do to start letting yourself feel more? Trust whatever arises.

CHOOSING YOURSELF

2025 is the year I decided to go all in on myself. My power, my magic, my messiness, my quirks, my crazy, my wild, my heart, ME. Fully, unashamedly.

I've been getting here slowly, showing pieces of the picture, fragments at times. But always knowing there was more I could be sharing, more I could be saying, more of me I could bring.

I'd see others doing it. Saying the thing I know I had felt before. Doing the thing I wanted to. I knew I had to go all in on me, I knew that is what I came here to do.

I know you are also here to do things in your way.
A way that's rooted in ancient wisdom and deep knowing.
A way that's aligned with your body and the Earth.
A way that's magical, intuitive, and wildly alive.
One that *remembers* we are all connected.

But ultimately, it's a way that is yours.

This will only happen once you choose yourself.
Choose to accept, welcome, and receive all of you.
The parts you once judged as too *something*.
The parts you locked away.
The parts you tried to tame.
The parts that you shamed.
The parts that you felt weren't enough.
The parts others judged as too much.

Let them out.
Give them space to breathe.

Get to know them, with openness, tenderness and curiosity.

It's time to choose all of you.

THE POWER IN THE PAST

There are so many parts of yourself you might have forgotten, parts that you've forgotten as you started to conform, fit in and belong. But also parts that you disowned as you maybe judged yourself at that time, or were judged by another.

As I was doing my daily chakra walks, and was nearing what this book wanted to become, I had clear guidance around each of my chakras rooting into different sites around the world, and in other star systems. Once they had done this, and I'd spent some time grounding, integrating and embodying it all, a younger me came along. She was me at around four or five years old, and she was completely in her power. She has this deep magical connectedness, rooted in the Earth but centred in the galaxies. Her sense of knowing who she was, unashamedly, without question, not caring what others thought, was palpable.

She then introduced me to some other younger versions of me, five in total, and they all nestled into one of the chakras that was rooted somewhere in the world/galaxy. This is who they were and what they each had for me.

My root chakra was tethered to Uluru in Australia and there came in baby me, just born. Even though she had just been given up for adoption, she was pure love. Only love. Here to bring love, be love and create more love. She reminded me that this is my power.

My sacral chakra was rooted in a pyramid under the Amazon somewhere in Peru. This is where four/five-year-old me was in her mischievous, miraculous fullness. She knows her power to create, to be, to choose what she wants. She knows that play and fun is key. She came to remind me that this is still me.

My solar plexus chose to connect into Atlantis under the ocean, and there eight-year-old me landed. She was the version of me that went through so much trauma when her mum died. So much change, so many shocks, so much disruption. This is when I began to lose who I was, to forget my power and the magic of life. But, she kept going. She did what she could, with all of her abilities. She's a fighter, she has so much strength, she never gave up. This is a part of my power, and sometimes we will go through shitty, unfair stuff. She showed me how she always believed, even though life 'happened' to her.

My heart chakra rooted into Sirius and that is where 15-year-old me showed up. She was so lost, so confused, had so much anger, didn't know where she stood. Her heart just wanted to love and be loved. The only way she knew how to deal with it all was to try and control herself through an eating disorder. She was so tender and vulnerable, but inside was hope. Hope that things would get better, that she'd find herself again. She reminded me to keep hoping. Hope is a powerful thing to have.

My throat chakra decided it wanted to root into the Andromeda galaxy, and 22-year-old me showed up here. This is a part of my life I have often judged and wanted to forget. I felt like a failure at life, living in a city (London) I just couldn't feel like myself in. I had been smoking a lot of weed so failed my art degree, which I have shamed myself for. But as I re-connected with 22-year-old me, she showed me how multi-dimensional, ahead of her time and magical she was. The world just didn't fit her. She was creating art projects that were about mass consumption being bad for the planet. She had insights coming to her around identity, belonging and home, that she was trying to articulate into things that could be monetised or in packaging that was marketable. But no matter how much she tried, it wasn't going to be the shiny, palatable, one-size-fits all approach that seemed to do well in the particular degree I was taking in art school. Today, I deeply appreciate her and love that I went through that experience as it was a reminder that my power is in not fitting in.

My third eye chakra connected into the Egyptian pyramids, and here 31-year-old me appeared. She was coming out of the worst year of my life – an absolute rock bottom, when literally the only way was up. She made the decision to totally overhaul and change her life, from the ground up. Day-by-day, choice-by-choice... she did. She transformed everything, so that life looked completely different less than a year later. Again, this was a time that I didn't want to remember. But it is thanks to 31-year-old me, in particular, that I am where I am today. Her inner knowing, her wisdom screaming that she *had* to do something, is what brought me to today. It's when I started listening to my intuition again, a huge part of my power today.

My crown chakra is connected into a golden pool at the core of the Earth, and there is me (as I write this) on my next birthday, a few months away. She's the mid-forties version of me who is a little further along than I. She has validated and encouraged me to keep going. We all need that inner cheerleader, even if they are just you a few months from now.

These younger (and one older) versions of me have all been doing their thing in each chakra. It's like they are a part of me, at home in my being. I'm sure there will be more that come and visit down the line. But for now, I'm so deeply grateful to each of them. The parts of me that each contribute a piece to my embodied power puzzle. The parts that make me who I am today, even if at the time I judged them, or felt at some of my lowest points in my journey.

I share about the places the chakras are rooted into as when I received these images and activations, they felt like a powerful remembering that we can also tap into power from different times, places, lifetimes – however you want to see it. Perhaps also the younger versions of me embody the gifts of these places too, and there's more to unlock?

If you want to begin to explore this for yourself, I invite you to listen to the visualisation 'The power of younger you' on my Insight Timer channel. Details are in the Resources section at the end.

NOURISH YOUR ROOTS

Roots hold us. They nourish us. They ground us in who we are, what we create, and how we move through the world. When our roots are strong, we feel steady. When they are tangled or undernourished, everything feels unsteady.

Deep, strong roots are essential for these uncertain times. They are non-negotiable if you are here to lead. I invite you to spend some time nurturing yours in the different areas of your life.

A few ways you can do this are:

1. Connect to you root chakra (at the base of your body) energetically in your body. There is a chakra diagram in the Resources section if you are unfamiliar with it.

What does your root chakra *look like, feel like, sound like, or even smell like*? I invite you to paint, draw, or create a visual (or even musical or culinary) representation of your root chakra. Let it flow freely – without expectation or judgement.

Step away, return to it after a day or so, and observe. What do you see? What do you notice about your root chakra from this perspective? What new insights does it bring?

I have some visualisations on my Insight Timer which will help you connect to your root chakra. Details are in the Resources section at the end.

2. Spend time connecting to your ancestry, for example the foods, the art, the creativity, or even the magic of your lineage. What are you drawn to be with and deepen your understanding and learning

of? Trust what comes to you and where you want to start exploring.

3. Spend time outside in nature with literal roots. Roots of trees, plants, flowers. Just be with the energy and trust that you are receiving what you need to. You could also create with them, paint them, photograph them, or even talk to or journal with them. Again, trust how you are called to connect.

DO-ING DRAMA

Stop do-ing, do-ing, do-ing.
Creating things to do.
Making things to do.
You don't need to *do* this.
You just need to be.

Deepen below the do-ing drama.
Into the essence of who you really are.
The current of your creator.
Where your life force flows with ease.
Where you'll remember your power is to 'be'.

WHO YOU REALLY ARE

Stop placing your worth, your value, your greatness, in others' hands and minds.
Easier said than done, I know. I've done it for literal years.

I dulled my sensitive needs and criticised myself for being too much, as the majority didn't feel everything so intensely as I. I let *them* dictate what I believed was right and wrong, so that I lost myself and my gifts, which are so rooted in my sensitive self.

I completely handed my worthiness over to men I dated – even more so to the ones that rejected me. I felt broken, not enough – why wasn't I chosen?

When I began a business I started to place my value in my audience. If they didn't buy from me, or respond when I shared, I'd feel utterly useless. Like a complete failure at business. Again, I felt not chosen.

As a child, before the world told you who to be, you likely *knew* who you were. The magnificent 1 in 8 billion brilliance that you are. The unique magical perfection of a being. This remembering is likely in there somewhere. Perhaps in a little corner, tucked away.

Finding it, nurturing it, nourishing it, fuelling it, is THE work.

It's your job now to remember who you *really* are.

THE VULNERABILITY IN BEING FULLY YOU

In a world built on constructs and identities that tuck you into a seemingly 'neat' little box, it can feel so tender and even scary as you begin to fully let this go and connect into the truth of who you are at your core.

The layers of protection... the identities... the constructs... Who the world told you that you are... It all begins to melt away. Even the deepest layers, that you didn't realise you'd built to keep you feeling accepted. Safe. To protect you. To keep your wholeness locked away.

All of it has to go.

This shedding can feel uncomfortable and bring up feelings of anxiety, fear and vulnerability. Deeper levels of vulnerability.

But as you do, you start to feel what is beneath it all. You begin to connect to your greatness and your magnificence. The truth of who you are, simply because you are a being, a soul, an eternal light.

You KNOW that this is who you are, but also questions arise:

'Is it safe?'
'Can I trust this?'
'Will I be okay?'

But, when you actually hold this energy, this knowing, this being-ness, and let it expand to hold you, because it is you and you are also it, you remember.
You remember the all-ness.

The peace.
The love.
The joy.
The overflow of sheer limitlessness and creative potential that you carry inside.

Your heart opens even more and starts to flood with love.
You remember your truth.
You are simply magnificent.
Each and every part.

All the things that were stopping you before fall away. You know that when you hold this energy, embody it and live from it, you can truly shift your reality.

You can be more YOU in the world; give more and receive more.

YOU ARE MAGNIFICENT

Do you know just how magnificent you truly are?
Your body is a fractal of the Earth's exquisite perfection.
The water in your blood came from the galaxies.
Your bones are made of stardust.
You carry the wisdom of your ancestors.
The gifts of your many lives.

You are a unique fingerprint in the fabric of time.
A cosmic coming together that happened at an exact moment.
A blessing of bloodlines colliding.
An explosion of beauty and truth.
You are truly magnificent.
Because you are you.

Water: Embodied Money

Money is integral to having more power on Earth. It is here to co-create with you and support you to make your vision real.

This section invites you to look at your relationship with money, alongside the frequency, flow and spirit of money, so that you can become partners, and welcome in money's current as part of your embodied power.

There are a number of spells, codes, frequencies, stories and activations which I received from communing with the spirit of *Embodied Money*. They are not included in any particular order, as this is a cyclical journey. I invite you to choose what you are drawn to and what you would like to embody more deeply.

MONEY, MONEY, MONEY

Oh dear money, how much in our world revolves around money! As I've mentioned in earlier parts, this book began solely with the focus on money. It's undeniable money is a huge contributor to having power in the world. It's not the only thing as I hope this book is a reminder of. But, it is integral.

When I began writing this book, my relationship with money was neutral, at best. For the most part it felt like a one-night stand where I'd receive money and then do my best to spend it, give it away, enjoy it, take all I could get. Then I'd be left scraping by, borrowing, going into debt, until the next injection came along. I'd get so angry at money. I'd feel it had abandoned me. Then I'd spiral and think that there was something deeply wrong with me for not being able to maintain a steady relationship.

The thing is, we're not taught about money in any way (or at least I wasn't – aside from basic maths using money). As I'm sure you are aware, so much of the way we connect to money is based on what we learned unconsciously growing up from our primary carers or other early influences. Then we have a whole lot of un-learning and new learning to do to create a different kind of relationship: the one we want to have, with money.

I have spent years, over a decade, working on this for myself. But it's only in the active process of writing this book that I truly began to feel this change. The frustration, anger and despair I used to feel if I'm going through a bit of a dry spell has gone. The impulsive, burning desire to spend everything the moment I receive it has gone. I love to hold money now, to be with it, to let it be in savings for a while. I love to co-create with it in a much more gentle, embodied way: seasonally and cyclically. I now deeply trust money, and know it will support me!

As a visionary leader you need money to make stuff happen. To create change. To support your mission. To support you.

I believe it begins with embodying money – and I hope the pieces in this section will inspire, activate and guide you into this.

DANCING WITH MONEY

Money asked me to dance. I said yes.

We swirled, we tangoed, we held on like young lovers... inseparable, ravenous for more. A hunger that couldn't be satiated. An entanglement that became one. Every desire and need had to be met.

The time came to part ways. We promised, in fact we declared, we'd always come back to one another. But as so often happens, time and distance changed us. We drifted apart – forgot what we once were. Forgot that familiar feel of being one and the same.

It now felt distant. Like we had never known one another. Had forgotten the other's smell. The soft cocoon of comfort that had once held me so well.

Would we ever dance again?

Money kept coming by. Knocking on my door. Waving at my windows. Wanting to start over. I didn't hear it. The music was always on loud. The busyness kept me distracted. I thought, 'there's no point, we'll never find a way back. It'll never be the same – I'm doomed to never dance again.'

But money never gives up. Money knows that one day I'll be ready.

It is always there knocking, waving, ready.

Saying, 'It is time to dance again.'

YOUR MONEY ROOTS

For months as I was journeying with *Embodied Money* I spent time with my roots in all forms. I'd already done loads of mindset and belief work around money. Literally coming up with as many stories, beliefs and thoughts I had around money that I could think of – then doing healing work to release, clear, heal, forgive, re-write, etc each one! I filled journals with the stuff! It was intense, heady work and it definitely shifted a lot for me.

But, as a multi-dimensional being who often lives in different worlds, I now realise it didn't go deep enough for me.

What needed to still be addressed and tended to were the ancestral roots I was still connected to, from my *many* lineages (I am adopted – so we're also talking the lineage of my biological, adopted, and step parents)… All of it!

I found that mostly it was tending to my roots through my biological parents, perhaps as I don't know much of their story, and so an assumption was made, as they were a lower-middle class Indian family. That, and the stories, memories, imprints carried in my bones, my blood, my cells from my physical ancestors.

It began with a deep craving for Indian food, which I suddenly started referring to as 'my roots'. Whenever I wanted Indian food, I would exclaim to my partner that I wanted 'my roots'. I have always loved Indian food, but this felt like a yearning, a hungry need for comfort and connection. I needed the food to ground and support me as I began to deal with a number of physical symptoms and what seemed like memories rising, from all in and around my root chakra area.

I started to feel money stories from the maternal side of my lineage rising. Times when money was taken away, or when there was no sovereignty or autonomy in earning. This would coincide with pain in and around my womb area – which would disappear as fast as it had appeared, after I had sat with the stories – acknowledging them, then letting them go in love.

Sometimes I chose to paint the emotions rising, especially if they felt vast, less able to articulate succinctly. I found that the paintings, once finished, often contained Indian patterns and motifs, and rich, bold colours – another connection to my ancestral roots.

This phase of deepening into the roots of money from my ancestry, and letting go of things on multiple levels – energetically, creatively and through my body – lasted a few months. Then one day, after a powerful tuning fork session, which likely cleared the remnants of things rising, I no longer felt it. Fascinatingly I also felt the yearning for Indian food completely gone. I no longer *had* to have it.

Whilst I was going through this experience, although I knew it was loosely connected to money and the book, I didn't really realise what was happening. It's only now in hindsight, and even more so as I write this, that I see the perfection in it all. How my body was also releasing and clearing – doing what needed to be done. So much emphasis when it comes to money is on the mind. So, of course with a book called *Embodied Money* (which then turned into a section within *Embodied Power*), the body needs to have its say too!

MUSING WITH THE ENERGY OF MONEY

I invite you to connect with the energy of money to begin to deepen your connection with it. You can simply call in money and see what comes to you. You could journal with it. You can also find a guided visualisation to support you on my Insight Timer channel – details are in the Resources section at the end.

Here are some of my journal entries when I connected with money, asking it 'What do you want me to know right now?':

'You are love. We are love.
We are one and the same.
We are on this planet to co-create together.
It's not about seeing money as something to obtain. It goes beyond that. It is a part of your life, your purpose, your existence.
When you begin to see it as such, with no separation, then you will truly get it, you will get money. Connect to what it is you want to do, who you want to be, what you want to experience, then let money come to support you.
You have to allow yourself to have what you desire, to be who you want to be, then anything and everything is possible.
It's an allowing, a receiving, an embodying of who you really are.

Let me in.
Let me support you.
Let me hold you.
You don't have to do this alone.
Let yourself be held.
Let yourself be vulnerable
Let yourself be exactly where you are.
Put down all the beliefs, stories, ideas, expectations and judgements.

Just place them to one side for a moment.
Now. Take a breath.
Breathe into your heart.
Let it soften. Let it fill up.
Let the walls, resistance and hard parts melt away.
Let your heart be held.
Tenderly, gently, softly.
Let it receive the energy of money.
It is safe to welcome it in.
It is safe to feel it, be with it, receive it.
Let yourself be with this.
Let your body soften into it.

Sometimes you simply need to go beyond your bank statement.
Open to the wealth of the world, of the Cosmos, of the possibilities.
Connect to feelings of freedom, support, spaciousness, beauty, rest, nurturing and gentleness.
Linger for a moment in this portal.
This is the key to feeling, receiving and embodying money.'

There were many days throughout my conscious journeying with money where I felt so much in lack. I felt anger, sadness, frustration. I felt fear rising around the amount of debt I was in with no knowing of how I would make the next monthly payments. I felt like my business was useless as I would put out offer after offer, to be met with a vacuum. I felt frustrated with the Divine, with Source, with being here on Earth.

I'd turn to my journal and say all of this to money. It told me to 'Recognise the joy, the expansion, abundance and overflow already in my life.' I was already living it. It also told me:

'You are here to do things a different way. To create, to be, to live from love. That is your currency. Love is money. Money is love. When you deeply and fully get that, things will change. Where are you not loving others? Where are you not loving what you do? Where are you not loving anything? Where are you not loving yourself? The energy of love and money is inextricably linked, and until you fully embody that, you block yourself from receiving it. Yes, others can receive it in different ways, but this is how you are here to. It has to come from love. Love. Love. More love.'

A DATE WITH MONEY

Imagine you are going on a date with money. Money is taking you out to get to know you, and you it.

Money knocks at the door.

How do you feel?
What are you wearing?
What do you notice about money?
How does your body respond?

How does money feel about you? Put yourself into its shoes, looking at you through that open door.

It's a beautiful warm evening; money is taking you to a restaurant with your favourite cuisine. You sit across the table from money. Taking it in. Being fully present with money.

What do you say to money?

What does it say to you?

How does the date go?

Reflecting on what came through for you from this exercise, how did it feel to 'date' money? Where do you notice you might need to make some changes? How about when it comes to money's perspective on you?

When I first did this exercise, I was quite surprised by how money felt about me! It was tentative, uncertain; it thought I didn't want to have much to do with it.

Even though I was initially surprised, it made total sense and it shifted something big for me. I started to spend more time with it, to get to know it, to show it I *did* want it to be around. I started to see magical money coming in – we're talking the totally random things like payments you'd forgotten years ago coming in, finding banknotes on the ground (which was my first time to even find money on the ground in Kenya) and random payments in my bank account.

TRUSTING MONEY

From my own money mindset work, working with clients on money, and the many, many courses I've done on money, I know it's not uncommon to have some core money 'blocks'. By this I mean core themes within your beliefs around money that arise again and again. Perhaps you'll spiral into a deeper layer of one, or gain a new perspective on something that you thought you'd dealt with.

One way to begin to tune into this is to ask yourself: 'If I had X amount of money right now (X being the abundant amount you desire), what would I feel?' Then allow all the thoughts, the beliefs and the stories to rise. Things like, 'I'd be happy, rich, free'. Then things like, 'But what if I lose it all or it gets stolen?' or 'But that isn't possible for me'...

Let all the thoughts come up and out – write them down ideally. As many as you can think of. Leave it a few days (or weeks) and let more bubble up.

The next step is to do some mindset work to release and re-write these beliefs, to align with a new, empowering way of relating to and with money. (There is a process for doing this work with limiting beliefs in the Resources section at the end.)

Some of the things that you wrote down you might be able to dismiss easily, *knowing* they aren't true. But others might be more complex and layered, and this is often an indication of the deeper, core ones that might need some more tending to.

Some of my recurring money 'blocks', which were rooted deeply into my psyche, were:

- It's safer not to have money, then nobody can take it away from me. I don't want to feel responsible for others or have more commitments, and always be asked for money.
- I won't feel guilt for getting to live a more joyful, creative, magical life than the majority of the world, especially people I love and care about.
- I deeply value my spaciousness and if I have more money it might mean having to do more, or feeling like that will change.
- I don't know if I fully trust myself with money, as I've often spent it all or given it away, as fast as possible. What if I do that and it all runs out, then I am left worse off than before.
- I'm not sure I fully trust money.

This is what it fundamentally came down to – feeling safe and learning to trust money.

So, to begin to connect to this, I asked myself these questions:

What would it feel like to trust money? To always have money flowing in, supporting me? What would I be feeling, thinking, being, doing etc?

I feel a softening in my body. I feel a relaxing; a letting go into the being-ness. I feel the slight sting of tears rising as I let go of all I've been carrying and trying to control. It's okay, I am safe, I am held. I've been clawing on to the fear of not having money, having to hustle, grind, 'prostitute' myself, do things I don't actually want to, carrying stories, patterns, beliefs. But if I just put that all down for a moment, and lean into the possibility of trusting money, I feel like I can breathe again. I feel like I can be me. I feel deeply connected to all that is – infinite intelligence, wisdom, and support.

What do I need to feel safe to let money in?

I need to feel free to choose what I get to do with money. I need to not feel obligated or burdened with responsibility. I need to feel like I won't be harmed and it won't be stolen from me.

Ultimately it's up to me to support myself to feel these things, so I asked for help, for guidance from my wise inner self, and I was reminded: I always get to choose. So often we feel like we *have* to do things, especially for others, as this is how we are raised. If we don't – we'll be judged or considered bad. I certainly was. But, at the end of the day: *I get to choose. I get to choose. I get to choose.*

When it comes to not being harmed or having it stolen – there was a little girl inside of me who had visceral traumatic memories of money being stolen from my parents by my caretaker. I loved her and she was let go for stealing, which broke my heart. Little me needed reassuring, holding and acknowledging that I will look after her, and no matter what happens in the future, I'm here for her.

FEELING SAFE TO LET MONEY IN

Do you actually feel safe having more money? Or the amount you think you want? It's all well and good to say you want a certain amount, but does it feel safe to have it in your body?

I invite you to tune into this.

Picture the amount you want – then imagine having it. It's yours – right now. Perhaps it's in your bank account. Or imagine holding it, having it right there with you.

Start to notice how your body responds. What thoughts come up. How do you feel?

It might surprise you what starts to arise, as your body, your being, isn't necessarily used to this amount.

You might feel fear: of the power it'll give you; the responsibility; that it will be taken; that you won't know how to manage it – you'll mess up.

The list goes on.

Just be open to whatever comes up.

Let your body start to tell and show you.

This is where the 'work' is. Starting to feel safe to welcome it in.

Keep connecting to this amount, the energy of it, the feelings that come up – keep sitting with it, being with it, holding it, letting your body get used to it.

This will begin to re-wire your nervous system, and your being, through repetition, so that your body gets used to this amount of money. This will make it much more likely you'll be able to hold this amount *when* it comes in. Not want to get rid of it because it doesn't feel safe.

HOW DO YOU WANT TO FEEL?

What do you actually want your relationship with money to feel like?
When you receive money, how do you want to feel?
When you spend money, how do you want to feel?
When you give money, how do you want to feel?
When you save money, how do you want to feel?
When you create or open to new ways to receive money, how do you want to feel?
When you think about money, how do you want to feel?

What does the powerful, sovereign, wise part of you say? How does *this* part want to feel?

What would it feel like?

What would it feel like to have all the money you desire?
What would it feel like to have money flowing in, from expected and unexpected sources?
What would it feel like to *know* how easy it is to make and receive money?
What would it feel like to never worry about money?
What would it feel like to live in financial overflow and abundance?
What would it feel like to give freely, generously and abundantly?
What would it feel like to live in deep union with money?
What would it feel like to know how supported you are by money?

What would it feel like?

BODY BELIEFS

When it comes to money work – so much focus is put upon money mindset. Uncovering the beliefs, the stories, the patterns that we have taken on, often in childhood (but also in later years, in past lives and through our ancestral lines). The work is then about holding and healing these beliefs – through re-writing them, healing the origin point, or simply choosing to believe something else. *This is deep, necessary work and if you haven't done it, it can be a game changer. In the Resources section is an overview on how you can do this mindset work if you are called to it.*

But, what about body beliefs?

One of the first things I was guided to do as I began to actively co-create this book (known to me as *Embodied Money* at the time) was 66 days of yin yoga (a slow, floor-based practice that involves holding poses for 3-10 minutes to deeply, but gently, stretch and lengthen the body's connective tissues or fascia. It has a meditative focus, helping to quiet the mind and release stress) where I would talk to a part of my body about money.

Some days were quite active and lots shifted and moved as I spoke with my body. Others were just about being in my body, present to all sensations.

My whole body had something to say about money at some point. Initially the things that came up were around out-dated beliefs and stories, which needed healing and holding. Once this had happened my body started to speak to me more generally and begin to show me its power. Power that has always been there. Power that can support me.

It truly shifted my relationship with myself, with money and my own power from the inside out.

If you are into yin yoga, or curious to explore it and what might come up, I highly recommend this practice as a way of deepening your relationship with your body and its guidance. You could start by setting an open intention to allow your body to share whatever it wants you to know. Or you could guide it more and ask 'What do you want me to know about money? Or power?' and then allow your body to show you. A certain part will make itself known, calling for your attention in some way, through sensation – so you do need to be present in your body.

In hindsight I realise this is often the work I do with clients – it was just so magical how my body took me into it for myself, without my conscious awareness!

Here are a few of the journal entries I made to show the progression and shift in what arose.

DAY 2

I was called to go into my hips. Specifically the right one. I felt the energy of society's expectations, whether real or perceived. "You have to be the best. You have to be good at all of it, or you won't be worthy of love, you won't be wanted." So, having pain in my hip is like a distraction and a protection from all of that. All I want is to be free to be me. My left hip doesn't feel the pressure so much, but there's a disconnect between the two sides. The right has to perform well, treats things like a competition (from my childhood conditioning). A dragon came in to transmute all of this energy of expectation. I get to be exactly as I am. I love me exactly as I am. I am free to be me; however I choose. There's a bubble surrounding me in all my quirkiness now. The pull from outside opinions released. This is who I am. I get to be free to be me.

DAY 9

My elbows got their turn today. At first I felt how they've been holding on so much! So tightly. If they didn't they'd miss out, get left behind, be left alone. They wouldn't be one of the cool kids. I encouraged them to let go, to be. They softened and relaxed a bit. With a little more time they really started to relax into the being-ness. Even languishing in pleasure! I saw lots of flowers and berries around them. I then asked about money and there was fear, lack of trust. If they don't push and work hard money won't be there. Money told them it wants to be friends, to give them more pleasure and joy. They don't quite fully believe it... yet. So money is holding them, and they are gently getting to know one another, learning to trust, building a supportive, dependable relationship. Watch this space.

DAY 18

My womb space is fucking angry. Furious in fact. Her power, her beauty, her sheer epic-ness has been ignored for too long. "Don't *they* know how fucking power-full I am? Don't they know I can create fucking worlds. Lives. Anything and everything. I'm fucking tired of being reduced to a monthly burden, or only wanted when they need me to create a human for them. Fuck that shit. I'll show them who I really am. Don't they know I am beauty, power, Divine intelligence. I don't have to do anything to prove myself. I just have to be me. I'm going to fucking show you. No more hiding, playing it safe. It's time to unleash the real, true me!" I feel a burning in my throat as these two portals of power unlock and truly become their selves.

DAY 25

My head is sore; it's calling as it is trying to control... take charge... be the part that keeps me safe, looking out for everything. It promised young, scared little me that it would. I spoke to my head: "I'm so sorry, my dear, beautiful head; I love you and I am so grateful for all you've done. I thank you so much. But now, it's okay to let go. What if I told you we are safe; we can't get it wrong. We're here to create magic and miracles now, but I need your help to do that. I need your powers to get on board with that, to do it with me. To bring in money, magic, love, joy and all that we desire to create and play with on Earth. I need you. I want to have fun with you now. You are magic, dear head, and I love you – but can we please use your gifts as well to create an epic life now? Please." It's letting the words land. I can feel a soft re-wiring as it begins to allow this possibility in.

DAY 29

Holy fuck, my womb started to kill me. Again. It felt like the most painful cramps ever – so, so painful. I felt a lot wasn't mine. It was the lack of control my female ancestors have had over their creativity, sexuality, receiving, and choices they can make when it comes to their own bodies. This has come up before, but today it wanted to scream. I had to move, sway, rock and finally hold my sacrum up on a pillow so my womb could be stretched open to release. It did. I brought in a deep purple-blue and diamond white flame. I let it all go – through all time and space dimensions. It released; it transmuted into gold dust of the highest frequency. I then felt an orange flame begin to glow in my womb. The surrounding area is a bit tight still – but lots is still moving, shifting, releasing. It's creating more space to receive.

DAY 55

There's definitely a shift in energy today! I feel a sense of peace within. A deep knowing and remembering embodied and re-activated as I step into the truth of who I am; on another level to how I've recently been living. I feel the deep holding, support and guidance of it all: money, the Universe, Gaia, the galaxies, my body. I feel to bathe here in this energy, in this knowing. To let it sink into every single cell in my body so it can remember this truth. It's a little later in the day and I fell into an old over-eating pattern, as it still feels like I haven't fully integrated allowing the good stuff in…

Letting it be good. I felt so full and bloated after. There was a little disappointment, but it wasn't too bad. Every day I'm learning and growing and being kinder to myself, and that is enough.

DAY 63

Truly feeling my power as a creator! My power in life. What I choose for me, for my life, how I live. All of it. I know the connection and energy I now feel daily with money is integral to creating a shift in my physical reality. How I feel the energy in and around – all the way from my crown to the tingling in my root, in my toes, and all the way into the Earth. I can now say I have a deeply magical, co-creative, supportive, abundant, overflowing, nourishing and flourishing, loving relationship with money. I just DO. I can feel it in and with me, holding me. I am money. Money is me. It's a deep love for one another, as I love myself it is reflected in all my relationships. And so it is.

DAY 64

I felt aligned and I took action on some things. Definitely a shift. I also love how I can keep connecting to and calling in my power – which feels like this deep support and a connection to my whole self. It feels so strong. I have a little nervous-ness and anxiety rising as I 'share' from this new place. Something is rising around claiming it and being able to own it. I know I can and will. My intuition has also got so acute, it's like everything has been heightened. I also feel a deep relaxation around money, a KNOWING it is here to support me, play with me, co-create with me. I love it. So grateful.

CANCELLING CONTRACTS, CORDS AND COMMITMENTS

What vows, cords, contracts and commitments are you still connected to, stopping you from receiving the financial flow you desire?

Is it a vow of poverty from a past life (perhaps as a nun or a monk)?

Is it a cord of commitment to your family, to never be richer than any of them, especially not your parents or elders?

Is it a promise you made to yourself as a five-year-old, when you saw, felt and created a story around the bad things money can do? You declared it then; you don't want to ever have lots of money.

Is it a commitment to yourself that you'll always choose love and happiness over money, because somewhere along the way you decided that you can't have both?

You might not even know what these contracts, cords, commitments and connections are. Allow these suggestions to bring up things – don't judge what arises.

Then declare it now, feel it in your heart, feel it in your entire being, speak these words aloud:

'I release, burn, dissolve, declare null and void, all contracts, commitments, cords and connections whereby I am giving my financial sovereignty to the power of another, in this and in any other lifetime – throughout all time and space dimensions. As of this moment forward I choose to allow money to enter my life through all means – known and unknown. I welcome money and know that how I choose to use it, share

it, save it and give it, is by no means a reflection of anything that others' do. I am in control and will use it for my highest good and the highest good of all. It is done. It is done. It is done.'

Feel a white flame dissolving all the cords, contracts and connections, burning away any energies that are no longer yours to carry.

Claim back your power to choose your relationship with money from now on.

THE CODES OF MONEY

It seems that some people can unlock money codes. They seem to have effortless income streaming in. They live in abundance. They don't worry about it. They create it as easily as they breathe.

I get that privilege plays a huge part in this. I get that there are nuances and it's not so black and white. But what if, for a moment, you let all that go, and let yourself play in the portal of possibilities.

What if you let yourself believe…

That you too can unlock the codes of money by aligning with the frequency you came into this world with. Not the frequency that you began to attune to through lived experience.
But the currency of creation, the vibration of the Universe.

Close your eyes for a moment. Go back in time, before you came into this body – in the space between worlds, where the Universe hums, where you are everything all at once.
Feel it. Connect to it. Remember it. Be it.

Draw that energy into every cell in your body. Let your body get to know it, flirt with it, tango together.

Slowly, maybe faster than you think, you'll start to remember that this is who you *really* are. This is who you came here to be. This is the energy you can embody in this world, if you choose it.

It starts with you.

There is a guided visualisation, 'Connecting to the time before you were born' to feel into this, on my Insight Timer channel. Details are in the Resources section at the end.

WHAT DO YOU MAKE MONEY MEAN?

If you have lots of money, what do you make it mean?
If you have no money, what do you make it mean?

If money comes easily, what do you make it mean?
If money comes rarely, what do you make it mean?

If you spend all your money easily, what do you make it mean?
If you hold on to your money, what do you make it mean?

Money isn't here to judge you.
Money isn't here to give you rules.

Money can come in with the certainty of a new dawn.
And just as swiftly, it can all be gone.

It doesn't mean anything.
It doesn't mean a thing.
So stop making it mean something.
When it's nothing at all.

THE GIFT OF MONEY

Stop seeing money as transactional.
Something you can make off someone else.
Something that has to come from someone else.
Yes, those things are true – but that root, that energy is not embodied.

See the quality of what you have to offer.
The miraculous-ness of how you deliver it.
The power of what you are bringing to the world.
The beauty of what it will do, create and activate.

Let money be the gold dust that carries your gifts.
Let it be the gift you receive in exchange for what you give.
See it for the magical vessel it is.
Like how you viewed it as a child.

You knew then.
You felt it then.
You knew it was something special.
Something to be deeply appreciated and valued.
Respected.

Value it as sacred.
Know it as a gift to be treasured.
Shift how you see it.
Feel it.
Receive it.

And watch what then unfolds.

TAKE RESPONSIBILITY

Take responsibility for your finances – your relationship with money.
Where it's coming from, where it goes, what you do with it.

Take responsibility for what you would like this relationship to be from now on.
How you want to feel, what's worked and what hasn't.

Take responsibility for creating a new financial reality.
One where you claim your sovereignty and power to do this.

Take responsibility.

THE LINK BETWEEN MONEY AND WATER

A mentor once pointed out to me how often we describe money using water analogies:

- Currency
- Floodgates
- Dry spell
- Dried up
- Leaking
- Overflow
- Bank
- Income stream

This observation stayed with me. Why *is* money so often spoken of in water terms? Why *do* we describe financial flow the way we talk about the ocean, lakes, rivers, rain or drought?

It made me wonder what else do these metaphors apply to? This is what came instantly:

- Creativity
- Love
- Power

At the core, all of it is energy.

This insight deepened my desire to explore the energy of money, not just intellectually, but energetically. To unlock flow. Dissolve blocks. Open the channel. And often, it doesn't start with money at all. It begins with expanding your capacity to receive and move energy through your body and life.

I share more of my own experience in the next piece, 'The frequency of money', but here are a few questions to help you start tuning into your own energetic flow:

- Where is my energy blocked or sluggish?
- What would help shift that?
- How can I open to more flow: physically, emotionally and/or spiritually?
- What would it feel like to be the most energised version of myself?

THE FREQUENCY OF MONEY

I've often reflected on the times I've received unexpected, significant sums of money. Moments in my business when I put out an offer, heard nothing for weeks, then suddenly three people want in at once. Times when items in my shop sell out overnight, even though I haven't been promoting them. Or when I've woken up to surprise payments. A large tax rebate. A gift from a relative I wasn't expecting.

You could say these moments are random. But the part of me that loves to track patterns has noticed something: these periods of sudden income almost always coincide with times I've been intentionally focusing on my *physical* frequency.

By that, I mean what I've been eating and drinking, or more accurately, what I *haven't* been consuming. These aligned moments often happen when I've been juicing, fasting, eating mostly raw, living foods, and cutting out stimulants, refined and processed foods (and alcohol, back when I used to drink). Things that make me feel sluggish, heavy or low simply aren't part of the picture.

I've also been moving my body more: daily, sometimes more, in ways that feel good and get me into nature as much as possible. There's a clear focus on creating lightness and flow within my body.

Maybe I've built a belief that I call in physical money when I feel light, energised and aligned. It could be. But what I choose to believe is that it's *all* about energy.

When energy flows freely through your body, when you're open to the currents and tuned into the frequency of what you're calling in, you naturally align with your desires. My intuition gets louder and clearer, and taking action feels effortless, guided, and right.

Of course, there are many ways to open to abundance. Mindset work is powerful for many. But for me, my body is a key part of the equation.

The chakras alignment walks I did (which I talk about in the Preface) definitely contributed to opening to more energy and flow, and continue to do so.

This is something I am playing with more and more, and I share a little about this in the Embodied Magic section.

Disclaimer: Please don't make radical changes to your health without support from a qualified health professional.

FOLLOW THE FLOW

When things seem forced, stagnant, stuck, tense.
Like you've hit a wall.
It's time to step back.
Let go, let go, let go.

You're so used to fighting, pushing on, ignoring resistance.
You're making it hard.
When it really doesn't need to be.
Let go, let go, let go.

Loosen your shoulders.
Soften your back.
Stop carrying it all.
Let go, let go, let go.

Let water be your guide.
Choose the path of least resistance.
Move with the currents.
Follow its flow.

THE CYCLICAL NATURE OF MONEY

There's a deep ancient vein, woven within the very fabric of our existence. It's the essence of the Earth. Of Gaia. Her being-ness, Her body is a part of us, and our bodies are a part of Her. We are intrinsically connected through the very fact that we are here in physical form. As much as we try to control nature, control everything, as though we are separate and in charge, we simply cannot deny this connection.

It's a force that governs the growth of everything on Earth. The ornate cherry blossoms that unfurl every spring on lands further away from the equator. The succulent deep orange-red mangoes that burst into abundance once a year, right when the ending of the short rains meets the warmth of the December sun, in the tropics.

It's the heartbeat of life that adheres to the cyclical rhythm of creation. Life, death and rebirth. The seasons which are more typically referred to as spring, summer, autumn/fall and winter. The dry and wet season. Yin and yang. Night and day. Always moving, always flowing, back and forth, from one to the next. In and out.

Change is the only constant. A deep acceptance of this, intertwined with sinking into the qualities of each part of the cycle and flow, is what the cyclical nature of money invites you into.

To embody money, to be at one with money in the body, you have to accept your body's true nature. This is where the gifts of embodied money are fully received.

THE EARTH'S MONEY

It became very clear that this is a book deeply intertwined with the Earth. Her seasons and cycles, Her currents, Her fierce power, Her unconditional holding, Her abundance, Her wisdom, Her.

At the end of the day, a large proportion of the things money can buy in our current society come from the Earth's resources, or are literally a part of the Earth in some way. For example food, housing, clothes, cars, travelling experiences, lifestyle experiences... If you look at everything you have spent money on, or want to spend money on – it is in some way connected to the Earth. The only immediate exception I can think of is a coach/mentor you hire, where the exchange is in information, but even then how that exchange happens, whether in person or over the internet/telephone, there are resources from the Earth involved.

So, if everything comes from the Earth and is connected to Her in some way, why have we forgotten that? Why do we treat everything like it's infinite? Why do we constantly seek growth at all costs, especially in the business world?

The Earth's resources are finite. They renew and replenish, yes, but they do so naturally on a far slower scale than we care to even pay attention to anymore.

This is an invitation – actually, it's a rallying cry to honour money as a part of the Earth.

Earth Money.

It is time to lean into the cycles of money – the seasons of spring, summer, autumn/fall and winter when it comes to money and your relationship with it. It's time to slow down and give as much credence to the darker, slower, feminine, yin sides of money, as the active, masculine, yang has been given.

Following are some suggestions for how you could do this, ensuring you mix and match from each of the seasons. You could let this be governed by what season of the year it is, the season of your business or a particular offering, or base it upon which season you are in personally.

THE SEASONS OF MONEY

As I connected to the energy of money and how it wanted to approach each season, this is what came through for me. I invite you to do the same if it calls you.

Spring

- Money wants to play and try new things – new ideas, new income-producing activities
- Start investing
- Plant financial seeds for the future
- Set money intentions for the upcoming cycle
- Spring clean your finances, de-clutter, trust what this might mean for you right now

Summer

- Money wants to experience pleasure, passion, joy – all the good things
- Share, give and donate with joy
- Magnetise fast, welcome in windfalls
- Let yourself be more active in your income-producing activities

- Let money flow in and out with ease, like a hazy summer breeze
- Invest in yourself

Autumn/Fall

- Start to save, invest wisely, put some money aside for the winter
- Let go of income streams that don't feel aligned
- Do a money audit on where you are spending that it's time to release
- Celebrate your money
- Let yourself receive support – financial or otherwise

Winter

- Less spending
- More stillness
- Start to align with your upcoming money vision (doing the inner work where necessary)
- Let your savings and investments grow and root
- Appreciate and give gratitude

WISDOM FROM GAIA

The Earth's resources literally come from inside of Her, or are grown from Her – rooted into Her. Let this be where you look for your resources – your wisdom, your riches, your gold.

THE FOUNDATIONS OF EARTH MONEY

Money was always meant to be shared, flowed, circulated, spent. It was never meant to be hoarded and kept, saved away, or worse – used to create separation, divide and to inflate one's status and power. After all, you can't take it with you when you leave Earth.

It was always meant to be used as a current of energy for creation, for exchange and to easily share resources and commodities globally.

Things got pretty messed up along the way.

Rather than going into the details of what currently is, I seek to share what could be. What this is a return to, and a desire to be.

Money that is rooted in love, care, reciprocity, generosity and trust.
Money that comes because it wants to.
Money that is allowed to flow freely.
Money that gives with an open heart.
Money that recognises the humanity in all.
Money that acknowledges that value in every person.
Money that thrives on creative expansion and growth.
Money that honours the seasons of Gaia.
Money that knows when it's time to rest.
Money that knows then it's time to take action.

Money that honours the source from which it came: Gaia, Mother Earth.

NEW TO MONEY

What if you let go of everything you've ever 'known' to be true about money? All the thoughts, the beliefs, the stories, the limitations, the patterns, the judgements, the fears – all of it? What would then be 'true' about money?

One way to do this is to get out of your head, where all of this information usually originates and is stored, and bring your awareness lower into your body. You could connect to your heart if that feels good. But I recommend going lower:

I was shown we have a 'root heart', which is a heart in your root chakra that has the power to pump up and down from the Earth. Your root chakra (along with your Earth star chakra) is your connection to physical life on Earth, so it makes this experience more tangible.

I invite you to connect to the energy of money through the awareness of your 'root heart' (or heart if that feels better for now). Bring your awareness into this part of your body so you are answering from here, letting this part 'speak'.

Then ask the energy of money: 'What are you (*you* being money) here for?' Be open to how it responds – you might hear it, feel it, see it; you could journal, or maybe you'll receive guidance later.

These are some of the things that came for me:

Money opens doors.
It creates possibilities.
It makes things happen.
It's an activator.

It's a catalyst.
It wants to co-create.
It wants to grow.
It wants to grant wishes, make magic, fulfil desires.
It wants to hold and support you.
It wants you to be fulfilled abundantly.
It wants you to receive the gifts of Earth.
It wants to circulate.
It wants to play and dance.
It wants to experience pleasure.
It wants to flow.
It wants to move.
It wants to be shared.
It wants to be your friend.

Next, I was guided to replace 'it' with 'I' and make all the statements present tense. Here are mine:

I open doors.
I create possibilities.
I make things happen.
I am an activator.
I am a catalyst.
I co-create.
I grow.
I grant wishes, make magic, fulfil desires.
I hold and support myself.
I am abundantly fulfilled.
I receive the gifts of the Earth.
I circulate.
I play and dance.
I experience pleasure.
I flow.
I move.
I share.
I am my friend.

How do these statements feel now?

Do they feel true?

What could you do to make them real? This is where there might be some active work to do.

Sometimes it's just about using these new 'statements' as affirmations for yourself to begin to align with these energies, and allow yourself to be shown the way forward.

For example, if you took the affirmation 'I flow' and had phone reminders pop up repeatedly, or stuck it up on your wall (some of the ways I've worked with affirmations in the past), you might find yourself bringing more flow into all areas of your life. You might find that you loosen up, or say 'yes' more. You might bring more creativity into your life. It is limitless as to what might happen as you connect more deeply into what has arisen for you.

MONEY WANTS TO BE TOLD…

Money needs you to own your power.
It needs to know you have got this.
It needs to feel you are in control.

Money needs you to be in connection with it.
It needs you to tell it what you want.
It needs to know that it has purpose.

Money needs you to speak up.
It needs to be given direction.
It needs to be told where to go.

So, speak up.
Figure out what you want.
Get clear on what you will use it for.
And go ahead, let money know…

It's waiting to be told.

MONEY WANTS YOU TO KNOW…

You are worthy of it.

You are worthy:
Of the things you desire.
Of the dreams you keep close in your heart.
Of the wishes you planted as a child.
Of the seeds you've been tending to since spring.
Of the visions you hold.
Of the things you've not yet imagined.
Of a life that lights you up.
Of a world that that has your back.
Of a world where you can be you.
Fully.
Freely.
Unashamedly.
Wholly.
Abundantly.

KEEP BELIEVING

Is there a part of you that doesn't fully trust or believe that things will change?
That you'll create a financial reality where you feel supported and free.
Possibly, as your reality until now hasn't consistently proven so.

You have to believe it's coming.
It's more than trust.
It's faith.
A knowing that emanates from your core to your roots.
Unwavering and unshakeable in its commitment.

Keep holding the faith.
Keep believing.
Keep knowing.
Hold this from the inside out.
It will show you the way.

I AM MONEY

What comes up for you if you say out loud/write down this affirmation?

As I have said 'I am money' and sat with it, throughout my book writing journey, even before when doing 'work' on money, how I have felt has changed.

Here are a few things it's brought up for me.

In the beginning there was no connection. Or even a disconnection. The words just floated over me. What does that even mean? Feel like? Look like? I didn't know, nor did I really want to. That definitely tells you something.

It then became a little heavy. Like I was taking on all the responsibilities of the world, or at least those close to me. It felt a lot. Burdensome. Obligatory. Um, no thank you.

I have felt some sadness. All this pressure we put on money. It's just trying to help. To allow us to exchange. To create. To live.

It then started to feel expansive. It was a way to be more of me. To be all that I want to be. To be the magnificent being that I truly am.

This is the energy I truly believe is at the root of money. A current into our most expansive, expressed, aligned, embodied self.

If we have traumas and stories, these will of course cloud the potential for this, but it's still there hidden beneath it all. And this, is my invitation to you as you dive deeper into money, as you embody money. To be your most expansive, expressed and aligned self.

MAGICAL MONEY

It's so easy to forget that magic is real. The magic you felt in your bones as a child. The knowing you could create worlds, make things happen, live in a world of limitless possibilities.

Reality can hit that out of you pretty fast and hard. For some more than others.

But especially if your role models, your primary carers, your teachers, didn't believe in magic. Especially in a world that has demonised magic and all that can't be 'proven' with the naked eye.

Money is a part of the magic of this Universe.
It is a catalyst, maker of dreams, co-creator of visions.
It is source energy directly wanting to make magic with you.

We've just forgotten this truth, this essence of money.

If we remembered it, I believe we'd be more mindful, more intentional, more creative, more loving, more childlike and more us!

Air: Embodied Magic

This section includes tools, reminders, stories and activations of alchemy, magic and creation. It is by no means exhaustive, as it is based on my experience and the things I personally use to support me.

It's a reminder of the magic you have access to, to support you as a leader. To remind you that your unique magic is an integral part of you power, which you *get* to use to support you.

I invite you to use it like a magic book. Pick a page at random and let yourself lean into it.

THE GIRL WHO REMEMBERED HER MAGIC

In a time before times, somewhere in the galaxies where matter ceased to exist, there were a number of souls gathered, waiting, ready to come down to Earth.

Some had been before, many times. Others had been there less. They each had different missions, bodies and journeys ahead of them. They were all intricately and intimately connected. They knew they'd play a part in each other's human journeys at some point in their next incarnation.

They knew that as they began their lives in physical bodies they would soon begin to forget their vastness, inter-connectedness and part of the whole, to some degree. They knew they had to learn what it was like to be separate and far from their truth. But they also knew there would be signs along the way to help them remember, if they chose to see them.

As they began their physical lives in the warmth of the womb waters that carried them, one of these souls was a little girl, who was about to experience a whole lot. She knew she was going to be given up for adoption, to reach the parents that were hers. But as she began to connect with the mother who carried her she started to feel her pain, her sadness, anger and confusion around what was going to happen. She felt intimately connected to this woman carrying her and didn't want to leave her like she knew she had to.

But life went on and she was chosen by the parents she'd come to be with. Within a couple of weeks she had moved to a whole new continent and home. She felt safe, loved and looked after. She got to be the magical little being she knew she was. She could wish for something, choose anything and it would become real. She knew how powerful she was, how her magic (her thoughts, beliefs and words) could create anything. She also had a gold angel always with her who protected her. She spoke to dragons, fairies, elemental beings and creatures in the garden. Life was truly a rich experience filled with colour, play, creation, fun and pleasure.

Without even knowing how she knew things, she knew about energy and how she could use it to do things for herself. She knew we all have powers and we can all do the things she did – we've just forgotten.

But then tragedy happened and in an instant the little girl's life got turned upside down, when her adopted mother died. What was once technicolour turned to black and white. She tried to hold on to her powers, use her magic to change things, but it got harder and harder. There was a voice inside her head getting a little louder every day; letting her know that magic wasn't real. How could something that painful happen if magic was real, and she hadn't been able to stop it?

So she began to stop using her powers, she began to not trust them, not want them, not believe in them. She buried them. She stopped seeing her angel, the dragons, the fairies. They all slowly faded into the ethers, like whispers in the wind. Layers of life started to pile on top of the little girl's magic. Sadness, anger, fear all burying the magic, until it was as though it never even existed.

She went through years of hating herself, not knowing why she was here, or if she could ever change things, find a way to be happy deep down inside again. Then one day when she had decided she didn't want to be here anymore, she wanted out, she heard a familiar voice. It was a voice that had been there all along nudging her, guiding her quietly (sometimes more loudly) behind the scenes, but this time it screamed. It told her she was here for more. She had so much more to give and a mission to fulfil, although she had no idea what that was (or what that *really* meant). But she couldn't leave now and if she started to connect to the voice each day it would remind her and help her. It would guide her back to herself.

So she did. Day after day she listened. Doing the things which she was guided to and life began to change. It very slowly started to get better. The feelings of despair slowly turned into hope. The endless anxiety became fuel to make changes. The bitter loneliness dissipated as she learned to be with herself again.

Those days turned into weeks, months and years, and life *suddenly* looked completely different. The colour had come back, and she remembered!

She remembered her angel, her dragons, the beings who supported her. She knew they had never left her; they'd just been waiting for her to believe again. She felt her magic and creative power again – and this time she felt even more powerful and magical than before!

CLAIMING YOUR MAGICAL POWERS

It is time to unashamedly, unapologetically CLAIM all the powers you know you have. The ones you buried. The ones you've forgotten. The ones you've shamed. Start to re-claim them. The ones that live in your bones and your blood, passed on to you through your ancestors.

Here are some of mine to activate the remembering...

- I can feel, know, see and hear energies
- I can travel into multiple dimensions
- I can feel what is unsaid
- I can feel desires and dreams
- I can hold a deep, powerful, activating space
- I can activate people into what they *really* need, not just what they think they do
- I bring people back to themselves
- I am an activator of love, magic, power, wholeness
- I am a powerful creator: my voice creates, my heart creates, my feelings create
- My empathy shifts energies
- My intuition is deeply powerful
- When I choose something I know it is done
- I can connect to unseen beings and energies powerfully to receive their guidance
- My words and creations are spells

TENDING TO YOUR MAGIC

Do you tend to your magic?
Fuel it like a fire.
Spend time nourishing it, being with it.
Deepening your relationship.

Just like any other part of your life.
Your health, your friendships, your finances etc.
It also needs presence, connection and nurturing.
Time exploring, journeying and adventuring with it.

It wants to play with you.
Get to know you.
Feel your way together.
Grow your evolving relationship.

So that you remember just how powerful your magic is.
You know this in your bones.
Magic has *always* run through you.
It just needs tending to.

INTUITIVE MAGIC

As I reached the top of the steps I glanced briefly at the sign ahead of me showing which way to go to find each of the hotel rooms. Rooms 101-115 were left and 116-130 were on the right.

Before I could even register which way I should be going, a voice inside me clearly spoke: 'Go left'.

So I did. My partner following close behind.

As we got to about Room 109 my partner (who was following me) and I both realised we had gone the wrong way. We were in Room 120 and this way wasn't familiar, or even the way the sign had directed, as we'd already been up and down from the room a couple of times.

So we turned around.

As we got back to the steps, in front of us, coming around a corner up ahead was an E-N-O-R-M-O-U-S male baboon! One of the biggest I have seen.

As we were at the steps (rather than at the corner exactly where the baboon was – which is where we would have been if we had turned right), there was some distance in between us and we were able to quickly go down and call for someone to help scare it off.

These alpha male baboons can be aggressive and attack, especially if you get in the way of what they are looking for – food!

I am so grateful I have such a strong connection to my intuition and deeply trust it to guide me in life (and business), even when it doesn't make sense. This is something that I'm guessing you already lean into yourself if you are here. But if not, below are a few different ways I have connected to my intuition over the years, which may inspire you to harness and let this magical wisdom support you.

THE YES/NO GAME

Something one of my first magical guides taught me was the yes/no game. It's about asking your body to show you what a 'yes' is, and then what a 'no' is. This can be very subtle, and is about beginning to notice the nuances and what comes up in your body. For example you might feel a slight clenching in your belly for a 'no'. Or you might feel a little beat in your heart, or an expansive energy, for a 'yes'. Or you might hear a 'yes' or a 'no', coming from somewhere in or around your being.

Once you have received guidance ask a question that requires a 'yes' or a 'no' answer and let your intuition respond. Then follow that guidance as this is how you build up that connection.

JOURNALING

As a writer I love to journal (although I acknowledge not all do). I often use Julia Cameron's *Morning Pages* (where you free write three pages first thing every morning) as a way to connect into my deeper wisdom. By free-writing three pages of whatever thoughts you have rising, you get past the clutter of noise and into the creative, magical gold beneath. The act of getting through the clutter and allowing what wants to come up through the pen is powerful.

EVERYTHING IS ENERGY

These days I like to play with energy and tune into the energetic field of something to receive guidance. Ultimately everything is energy and so it's about tuning into the energy (or life-force, or Spirit) of whatever you want to know more about; and listening, feeling, receiving guidance from it. You can do this with anything, and I mean anything! I like to do it with things I am creating in my business, with books I'm writing (you can read all about this in the Preface section), also energies I am calling more of into my life such as the word 'limitless' or 'creativity'. Each of these words has a particular energy and guidance you can tune into. I have a few visualisations guiding you into this on my Insight Timer channel (details are in the Resources section).

Ultimately, we all have an innate ability to tune into our intuition (or inner wisdom/guidance) to receive guidance and deeper awareness. Connecting to your intuition is like having someone to support you with making choices or deciding what to do next. It really can support you in all areas in your life.

We all connect in different ways, and it's about experimenting and finding out (or even remembering – as you know how to do this as a child) the ways your intuition 'speaks' to you. Also acknowledging that how you connect to your intuition can change throughout your life – mine certainly has.

Connecting with your intuition is a practice. It is a bit like a muscle in the body and the more you use it, connect with it and listen to it, trusting what comes up (even if it doesn't make sense – especially if it doesn't make sense), the stronger it gets.

WHEN IT DOESN'T MAKE SENSE

I had this gnawing feeling in my belly to cancel a workshop I was running. It was on a Friday afternoon and aside from it being complimentary to members of my Embodied Business group I run, nobody else had signed up. I didn't want to cancel just because of that, I like to show up and follow through. Plus it was on grounding which I knew would support me too. But, I couldn't shake the feeling that I was being guided to cancel.

My partner's mum, (who I have known since my teens and was very close with) had been unwell for a long time, and that week she'd been feeling worse. I had been planning to see her on the weekend, but I had this feeling that wouldn't leave me that I had to give her a hug that Friday. So I cancelled the workshop and went to see her. She seemed smaller, frailer, but still her – always welcoming, smiling, chatting, wanting to know how *you* are!

I got to give her a hug. In fact she wanted more than one. I told her how I remembered one time in my early twenties when we'd been a bit drunk together one New Year's Eve at the beach, how she'd told me I would always be a part of her family and really made me feel it. At the time I was going through a lot of issues with my own parents. It was something that made me feel so held, wanted, and has always been in my heart, making me love her even more. I told her how much that moment meant to me, and that I was so grateful to be back in her life all these years later. Before I left we talked about what I could cook for her, and about arranging some gentle healing sessions.

But the next morning her soul left.

I am so beyond grateful I listened to my inner nudges. It's something I could so easily have ignored, but I listened. The old me would have definitely chosen work, or anything work-related, over *anything* else! But instead, I got to have those last few special moments with her. And whilst I still feel all the waves of grief, heartbreak and all that death brings up, I do feel a sense of closure and such gratitude, as it was so Divinely guided.

TIMELINE JUMPING

Timeline jumping is a powerful practice for consciously aligning with a reality you desire, one that already exists, even if you're not currently experiencing it. At its core, it's the understanding that there are infinite parallel timelines unfolding simultaneously. Somewhere out there, right now, there's a version of you already living, being, doing, embodying the thing you're calling in. Whether it's a relationship, abundance, a creative project, a way of life – it's already real for them.

Timeline jumping is about opening yourself to that possibility, stepping beyond the limits of the rational mind, and tuning into that frequency. You're not *making it happen* from scratch. You're aligning with what's already true in another reality… and anchoring it here.

As you connect into different possibilities and versions of yourself, you become aware of hidden aspects. Character traits, qualities, ways of showing up, ways of being that you can now embody, so that you become this version faster – thus collapsing time.

You can also use timeline jumping to gently edit or shift your current reality, choosing a version of events, patterns, or experiences that align more deeply with your highest good.

My preferred way to access this is through guided visualisation, letting my body and energy field feel the shift. But it can also start with journaling.

Here are a few prompts to begin activating your next timeline:

- What's the one thing you're most ready to shift in your life right now?
- When you tune into your current experience in this area... what feels heavy, misaligned, frustrating or limiting?
- What would it mean, on a soul level, to transform this?
- If this area of your life felt exactly how you desire it to... what would be different? What would it feel like? Look like? Sound like?
- Now... meet the version of you who is already living this.

    What are they like?
    How do they move?
    What do they prioritise?
    What do they no longer tolerate or engage with?
    What beliefs or ways of being are natural for them?
    What's the frequency and energy of their life?
    What does it feel like?

Let your body start to receive them fully. Let it sink in. Let it become familiar. Because the more familiar it feels, the faster it anchors.

I played with timeline jumping to write this very book you are reading. To do this I was connecting to the timeline where I had already written the book; really feeling, seeing and holding it as done. I could feel the finished book, its energy, its magic. I could feel the 'me' who had written it. She actually had shorter hair and was feeling much more confident and assured than I was at the time. Funnily enough, without even consciously realising what I was doing, I had my first haircut in months a few days before this book was complete, and when I looked in the mirror I realised I had become that version of me. Book written and all!

I also used this technique (after doing a lot of deep, layered work around self-worth, receiving and relationships) to call in my current partner. A man I'd secretly held in my heart since I was a teenager, someone I always felt an inexplicable, undeniable soul connection with. Back then, I couldn't even articulate it. It was just *there*. For years, it felt impossible. We lived on completely opposite sides of the world, we each lived different lives, were in other relationships.

But everything shifted when chance had us back in Kenya at the same time (initially only for a couple of months – we both had plans to return to separate countries), and I felt the connection stronger than ever so chose to consciously create the relationship I truly desired… So I anchored into the timeline where it was not just possible, it was inevitable. The version of me who believed it was available became the portal, and it happened. We stayed together in Kenya, now over two years later (at the time writing).

I have a mini timeline jumping bundle including visualisations and a workbook guiding you into this if you want support. Details are in the Resources section at the end.

IT'S TIME TO COME OUT OF HIDING

You are a bridge between the worlds.
You navigate the edges with your multi-dimensionality.
You are a keeper of ancient wisdom.
You are a portal into the unknown.
Your gifts are rooted in this paradox.
Your essence is found in this acceptance.
It is time to be your whole self.
Let the pieces you've been compartmentalising out.
Let the world see you in your fullness.
It's time to come out of hiding.

ALCHEMISING THE PAST

You have the power to alchemise.
Stories, patterns, beliefs, feelings, emotions.
Anything it's time to let go of.

Hold them, be with them, honour the part that they've played.
Then let the current carry them out.

Release them as tears.
Express them through rage.
Move them through your body.
Paint them.
Create them.
Write them.
Speak them.

Call in the elementals.
Work with your guides.
Let the angels help you.
Harness the energetic fields.

Let the process change you.
Transform you.
Re-birth you.
Again and again.

Transmute the energy into magic.
The spark of a creation.
The essence of your becoming.
A leader who embodies their wholeness.

RETURNING WHAT'S HERS

Golden, shimmering pebbles plopped into the murky lake waters. She was throwing them in one-by-one. Tears stained her cheeks.

This was the only place she could find peace, away from the expectations, the duties that She, their only Indian daughter, must fulfil. It was how it was done.

I walked over. She knew me. I knew Her.

Memories flooded my ears, of being brought to this very place while She and I were one. Her singing to me. Words of catharsis, joy, love, shame, despair, all of it. We spent a lot of time here together.

She never wanted to give me up. She wanted to run away, to raise me, to live a life of creative freedom with limitless possibilities. But it hadn't happened that way. Fear. Money. She didn't want to lose that support.

It was time to give back what was Hers. Her anger at not being able to pursue Her heart's calling. Her fears. Her life.

She held my left lower back and I could feel the energy being drawn out of me. Returning.

I know my creative spirit comes from Her, and from Her grandmother – my great grandmother. *"Live that life,"* She said. *"Nurture your creative heart."*

I woke up.

This was a visualisation journey in which I returned some of the beliefs and fears I had absorbed from my biological mother. Ones that were never mine to carry. You too may have taken on stories, patterns or emotional imprints while in the womb. This is incredibly common as information travels through water, and as developing beings, we absorb so much.

I invite you to explore this for yourself. Gently ask, *"What did I pick up in utero that is no longer mine to carry?"* You might journal on what arises or explore it through a regression practice.

ROOT REMEMBERING

There's an orangey-red flame glowing in your root. The remnant of a dream once dreamed. The thread of a story once told. The wish of a vision once imagined.

It's there. Still flickering. Still alight. Still holding on.

This flame is a reminder of the part that knew. The part that came into this world with a knowing, a dream, and a force to be reckoned with.

The part that knew anything was possible. Magic was real. Miracles happened. And that was the way it would be.

When it was time you simply had to speak the words, invoke your spell, cast your magic and it would be done.

But life got in the way. Things happened. You were told no. That's not possible. That's not real.

So you forgot. You stopped believing. You let the fire burn down.

But somewhere still inside your root, there's a remembering of that way. The power you carry, the knowing of what's possible.

The flame is there to remind you.

Can you feel it?

THE HEART OF THE ROOT

On my many walks connecting into my chakras, I kept feeling and receiving the message that the root chakra has a heartbeat – a pulse that connects to all life on Earth.

*The root is the portal through which we enter the world (unless we're born by C-section) and it's the chakra where we begin to form our sense of safety, belonging and home in the world, in the first few years of life. It seems to me, that there **must** be some kind of connection to a heartbeat here, as it's when the heart stops beating that life in the physical ends.*

I started consciously connecting my root chakra to the Earth. When I would go for walks in the Kenyan forest I would always stop to sit on the Earth. Feeling that root connection. My root then began to draw up the golden honey-like currents and energies from the Earth's core. From there my root, just like a heart, could pump it into and around the rest of my body.

I could draw up creative power, or strength, soothing, nourishment – whatever I needed that day.

You can do this for yourself, by imagining your root chakra growing roots down to a place you would like to connect to e.g. somewhere in the world; the Earth's golden core; or even places like Atlantis or another galaxy. Then invite your root to draw up what it needs.

There's a visualisation named 'The creative power of your root' which will guide you to connect with this on my Insight Timer channel. Details are in the Resources section at the end.

UNLOCKING THE MAGICAL CODES OF YOUR ANCESTRY

What are the gifts of your ancestors?
The red thread of wisdom woven from womb to womb, through blood and bone.
The codes that you carry from the heritage of your lineage.
The hardships endured.
The battles won. The battles lost.
The insights gained from daily commune with nature.
The skills mastered through years of fine-tuning.
The perception received from the presence of being.
The knowing that needs no explanation. It simply is.

What magic runs through you from your ancestors?

THE HEART LOCK

In a power-full visualisation I came across a heart lock in my chest-throat area. It was a lock that contained all the things I unconsciously had chosen to keep from my biological parents and ancestors. It was the patterns and beliefs around lack. But also the gifts, powers and wisdom that came from them. It was my way of keeping a connection to them, of keeping a part of them inside of me.

I was guided to release the things I no longer needed, letting them be dissolved, alchemised and transmuted. But I am always connected through the things I chose to keep. Some of which were my innate chakras' wisdom, my deep connection to nature's magic and the power of my words.

We each carry an unseen lock within holding inherited patterns, beliefs and energies from our lineage. Some are rooted in lack or fear. Others are sacred gifts: ancient wisdom, elemental magic, natural powers.

To apply this in your own life, close your eyes and tune inward. Ask:

- What am I still carrying that isn't mine to hold?
- What ancestral gifts am I ready to reclaim?

Imagine a heart lock within you. See what lies inside. Let what's no longer needed dissolve. Keep what is sacred. This is how you honour your lineage while stepping into your own power.

THE POWER IN WORDS

Your words are incantations.
Your words are spells.
Use them wisely.
Use them well.

All your words have the power to create. Whether you think them or express them out loud in some way – whispering or shouting, it doesn't matter.

More and more throughout the writing of this book I was shown the power of my words.

I would randomly think about a food I was craving – such as one of my childhood favourites, banana crisps – then I'd be offered some within 24 hours, having not seen them around in months.

I love to play with my magic, especially when I am walking in the forest. I'll declare that I am going to have the forest all to myself and not see another person, if I'm in the mood for some serious alone time. Within a few minutes all the people I could hear clear out from around me and at most I'll only bump into one or two people the rest of the time I'm there.

I would say I wanted to eat Indian food and then be asked out to dinner that same day.

If I wanted a delivery to come at a certain time within a 4-hour window I'd speak it and about 99% of the time it would come when I wanted it to.

Another time I had a food delivery scheduled for later on in the day, and I remembered I had forgotten to order garlic. It was too late to add it, but it came in that order (by accident)!

So, the thing is I seem to be able to speak a lot of random things into existence, not so much the specific things I wanted when it came to money. I know that I have more attachment to this, so it's something I am working on.

I realise (for any cynics) that all of this is very closely linked to mindset work, where your reticular activating system has become aware of something so is bringing it to your attention. However, I *know* in my bones that we have the power to invoke and create through the power of our voice. So this is how I choose to see it. The more I claim and believe what I desire, the more it works out that way for me. Words truly are spells.

GET OUT OF YOUR OWN WAY

Sometimes we want something so badly that we end up gripping it too tightly, obsessing, over-efforting, pushing harder and harder, until we unknowingly delay or even repel the very thing we desire.

I've had a dream since the age of 17 (maybe even younger) to have my own home. Having my own space where I can retreat to, where nobody can tell me what to do, where I can decorate it as I choose, where I don't have to answer to anybody. Somewhere that is a sanctuary for my sensitive needs.

I have spent hours journaling about it. Writing it out as though it's already done. Creating many vision boards. I've even brought it to a 'Power of Eight' setting group, where you take it in turns to bring an intention that the group then focuses on to amplify the results. It's a dream that I have certainly put a lot of effort into and wanted *really* badly.

So badly, I often focused on the lack of it, and the contrast has been highlighted. In the four years before writing this book I moved over 22 times. I've lived next to generators that made my nervous system rage. I've taken phone calls from my bedroom, with traffic so loud, people thought I was standing on a highway. I've been reminded, constantly, of what I didn't yet have.

When I stopped trying to force it… when I let myself *be* at home in my own being… when I allowed myself to feel held and safe with my partner… home arrived. Effortlessly. An actual physical home was basically handed to me.

When I truly embodied the desire I was trying to receive, it came to me.

When you become the frequency of what you desire, it naturally comes closer.

Not from force. From resonance.

The more I got out of my own way, the more space I created for what was already trying to find me.

PLAYING WITH TIME

Something I've been doing more and more of is playing with time. We all know that feeling of time simply flying by if you are doing something you love. Or perhaps it taking for-e-v-e-r if you are bored and wanting it to go by quickly.

What I've been doing is invoking my power to make time feel and be how I want it to.

For example, I often do cleanses to help align my energy and so I can feel grounded and in flow with what I am creating (I shared a piece on this in the Embodied Money section). I used to see physical results materialise from these cleanses in approximately 3-4 weeks of starting them. One day, before beginning a cleanse to call in clients I thought I would play with collapsing time. What would it be like if one week was equivalent to one month, I wondered? I declared that this is what would happen and sure enough a new client, out of the blue, got in touch and signed up to work with me on day five of the cleanse.

This has also really worked for me recently as peri-menopause has changed my body's needs, and it currently feels more depleting than positive to do the longer cleanses I used to do in my thirties.

Another thing I've been playing with is extending time. So many people say that time seems to speed up when you get older. I used to agree with this. I've asked time to feel rich, juicy, abundant, and lingering with pleasure. So far, overall, I can say that the past three years have felt exactly this. So full and deeply delicious. Sure there have been some challenging and painful times within them – but I appreciate these parts for what they've also given me.

RE-WIRING YOUR SYSTEM

We're so used to not getting our hopes up, expecting the worst, training our brains to think that they need to play it safe. For our own protection, to not get hurt, to not feel disappointment.

But what if, instead, you did the opposite. Kept thinking, believing, trusting that the BEST is happening.

That the soul-aligned clients are coming. The people who need your work are on their way. People are booking you out-of-the-blue. Your leadership is changing lives. Everything is always working out exactly how you want it to.

Feel into that possibility for a moment. What does it feel like?

Let yourself really go there.

Let your body begin to feel it. To get to know it.

Linger here as long as possible. Keep going here, practicing it, even if the outcome isn't showing you this.

It's up to you to keep re-wiring your system, so it gets used to it.

So it feels safe.

So it becomes your new normal.

WATER WHISPERING

There's magic in the waters, frequencies that merely need directing.
Water can soothe, quench, soften and hold.
It can destroy, rampage and be bold.

Take a moment to whisper to the water in your body, the water you consume.
Thank it. Send it love and gratitude.
Let it know your dreams and desires.
Infuse it with your intentions.

Something I do is to write my wishes on little Post-its then stick them on my clay water filter to infuse the water I drink. I have a magical, creative friend who made coasters painted with the intentions of words like 'love', 'abundance' or 'joy'. These can then infuse the drink placed upon them with your intentions.

MORPHOGENIC FIELDS

I began playing around with morphogenic (or morphic) fields with money, but you can do it with anything.

Put simply, this is done by connecting to the energy field (which is an amalgamation of the energy of beliefs, stories, threads – anything at all that might be contributing to its make up; from yourself and the collective who also subscribe to and contribute to that field) of a way of thinking or being.

So, for money – I simply asked to be shown the morphic field I was currently connected to when it came to money. This is what I felt, saw, experienced...

To begin, it felt dark and hazy, like a weighted blanket. It felt safe to hide here, it accommodated my need to retreat (or at least that was the illusion). As I felt into it more deeply I could feel ancestral veins of a struggle. Difficulties and hardships being touted as a badge of honour. Having to suffer to survive, to simply belong. 'Clunky' and 'jarring' were the best words to describe the energy of it.

It felt like this morphic field was locked into my third eye and crown chakras. It was hard to energetically detach myself from it, but I called in my dragons to help me, and I unhooked from the tentacles of this energy field.

I then called in the money morphic field of abundance, limitlessness, ease and overflow. Almost immediately I was shown rainbow colours swirling in and out of me. It felt co-creative, magical, ripe in possibility. I felt how this field wanted to support me to be fully me. But before that I felt it saying *'For now, rest, look after yourself right now.'*

In the days, even weeks, that followed this connection, a lot more rose around the beliefs I was still tethered to. Most of it simply came up to be released, to leave my being, and I just had to let it – not judge it or myself. So please be aware that this can happen as you connect to these fields.

Today I can feel the magical morphic field more strongly, I just have to remember to connect into it and let my body receive it, which is part of my ongoing 'work'!

ENERGETIC PROTECTION OF YOUR SPACES

I've talked about looking after your own energy and sovereignty, but this also applies to the spaces you create, run and are a part of both online and offline. This includes your social media channels, the offers that you put out, the programmes or groups you run, the creations you release into the world. The talks or workshops you are part of. All of it.

This is a little reminder to claim the intention you desire for your spaces and creations, and set the field up for them. Some of the things I like to do are:

Set up an energetic field for new group programmes, by imagining a golden bubble of light surrounding them, only open to those who are ready for my work. I infuse the field with qualities that are a part of the programme and that form its foundation, such as colour, alchemy, magic, love, holding and power. I do this by simply speaking them into the field.

Sometimes I even create a physical touchpoint to have as both something I can use to call people in (to make some magic) and to receive it through my physical senses as I set up the field for it. For example I might paint the energy I feel of the offer I am about to share. Then I might have flowers especially chosen from the garden, which I place on top to represent the qualities and characters of the people I am calling in. I then will infuse it with the boundaries and energies I desire. After that I'll likely feel into it daily, deepening my relationship with it, whilst I am sharing about it and actively inviting people in.

I say a little incantation or prayer before I release something into the world, declaring that it only reaches those that it is here to benefit for their highest good.

I like to set boundaries on my social media and online spaces so that they only attract people who want what I am here to share, and who are here to connect in a positive and constructive way.

In a world where trolling and negativity is rife, the more I do this the safer I feel to share more of myself.

Trust yourself here – you know what to do. What would make your spaces online and offline feel supportive to you?

CHAKRA DRAGON CLEARING

I first connected to the chakra dragons when creating my *Embodied Wisdom* oracle deck. They came through right at the end and just *had* to be a part of it. They've stayed with me since, and whilst they took backstage for a while, they came back front and centre when this book was coming close to being complete.

I am a huge fan of chakra clearing and the magic within the chakras (see more on this in the Preface section). Something super quick and powerful you can do to clear your energy, ground you and step into your power is a chakra dragon visualisation. (If you are unfamiliar with the chakras, take a look in the Resources section for a diagram and brief explanation of the chakras.)

Every time I do this, I feel a surge of strength and deep-rooted power.

You can either do this exercise walking as a moving meditation (which is my preference these days), preferably out in nature, or you can be somewhere comfortable where you can sit or lie and you won't be disturbed.

Start to connect to the dragons at the core of the Earth, and then invite up their energy into your Earth star chakra beneath your feet in the ground. Invite it to clear, cleanse and activate it. Wait until you feel the energy begin to radiate outwards, then move up and do the same, bringing the dragons up to your root chakra at the base of your body. Once that is done move up to your sacral chakra near your belly button; then your solar plexus chakra at your stomach; then your heart chakra at your heart; your throat chakra at your throat; your third eye between your eyebrows and your crown chakra on top of your head.

Feel the dragon energy lighting up each chakra, fuelling you, strengthening and activating you. Keep breathing it in, being with it for as long as feels good.

If you want to be guided into this, you can find a 'Chakra dragon energy boost' visualisation on my Insight Timer channel – details are in the Resources section at the end.

KNOWING IT IS DONE

When I was a child I could choose something and I just knew in my bones it would happen. If I wanted to win a school drawing competition, be cast as a certain role in a play, or be paired with a friend in a group to work together – something in me just knew to choose it and KNOW it was done. It then materialised without fail. I guess you would call it manifesting, although I had no idea that was what I was doing. I just knew my creative power.

Later, as life happened and I experienced a traumatic event which changed the trajectory of my life (my mother's death), I lost touch with my creative power and knowing. I stopped believing that magic was real, that miracles could occur and that the world had my back.

But there were a couple of occasions that stand out where I tapped into that magic I still had.

I was in my first year of secondary school (that's aged around 12-13 years) and I had to do an art final for the end of year exam. I can't remember the theme, but I decided to draw a whole bunch of fruit. Up until this point my drawings were flat, they had no depth and looked a bit like colouring pages with flat colour inside. But something in me decided, CHOSE, in that moment for my art final that I was going to be able to draw this fruit exactly as it looked. Honestly it was like I shifted timelines, stepped into a current or flow that I wasn't in previously and embodied a different version of myself (whatever you want to call it). I picked up my watercolour pencils, had a shiny red apple in front of me and I drew that apple exactly as it looked. Depth, colours, form, shading – it was all there. From then on I could draw still life.

Another example from when I was a bit younger was when I was playing in a rounders tournament (a sport that uses a bat and has four bases). I was the reserve of the second team, as I hadn't hit a ball all season, so unlikely to be called to play. Something in me shifted that day again. By coincidence (or magic ;-)) I was called to play that first game, and I was the only one of two to score a rounder (which is hitting the ball far enough so you can get around all the bases, without the ball being thrown back – a bit like a home run in baseball). So I was kept in the tournament for the next game. I then found my flow, scored multiple rounders in every game and we almost won the whole tournament. I was named batter of the tournament!

I've reflected on these times where I simply chose what I wanted, and knew it was done. I've been able to replicate it more easily with some things and less with others. Often it's harder with the things we have more attachment to, like that launch you want to go a certain way, or the client or job you *really* want. The things that we have more healing or holding to do around, or layers of unconscious conditioning or blocks that don't really want whatever it might be.

It's choosing something and knowing it is done.

It's aligning with your natural flow and currents, and the currents of creation, money, energy, magic and miracles, so you feel this knowing in your bones.

MAGICAL TOOLS

I imagine you already have magical tools you're naturally drawn to whether it's astrology, plant medicine, working with spirit animals, or tending to the dreamscape.

And if not, I invite you to begin exploring what feels resonant. Start with the tools connected to your own lineage and heritage. And if you are working with practices that come from other traditions, cultures, or lineages (but also your own), my invitation is to approach them with reverence, honouring their sacredness, and tending to them with care, respect and integrity.

For me, this has been a very personal journey. As someone adopted at birth from India into a white Western family, I grew up disconnected from my Indian roots in many ways, but as a child, I was always drawn to colour and energy.

That deep, unexplainable connection soon led me to the chakra system, including the colours of each (which originates from India). The chakras became foundational in my life and are now woven through all of my work. This connection with colour deepened further as I trained in spiritual colour psychology (in the Colour Mirrors system) – a modality that brings profound insight and awareness to whatever you're navigating, by looking at the meanings of colours you are drawn to and repelled by.

I lean into the wisdom of my chakras on an almost daily basis alongside the guidance of my body as a whole. It's become one of my most trusted ways of attuning to what's true, what's moving, what's needed.

This work became so alive for me that I painted and wrote my oracle deck *Embodied Wisdom*, which draws on the chakras, colour frequencies and intuitive guidance from the body itself. These are the kinds of magical tools that don't just offer insight, they help you remember yourself.

Working with magical tools doesn't have to be complicated. It can be as simple as tuning in, listening, and allowing yourself to be guided.

You might:

- Check in with your chakras (there's a diagram at the end of the Resources section) to notice which parts of you feel open, constricted, under-energised or over-activated, and tend to them accordingly.

- Work with colour intentionally, by wearing, surrounding yourself with, or visualising colours that support what you're navigating (e.g., grounding with red or copper, softening or bringing in love with pink, activating clear communication with blue).

- Pull a card from an oracle deck, not necessarily for answers, but to open a dialogue with your inner wisdom (through what the card brings up in you).

- Sit quietly with your body and ask: *What do you want me to know today?* And then listen, notice, receive its wisdom however it wants to respond.

- Track the symbols that show up in your dreams or in nature: what are the animals, colours, numbers or patterns communicating to you?

- Use breath, movement or sound to shift energy when something feels stuck.

There's no one way to do this. The magic is in the relationship you build with your tools. The more you work with them, the more they reveal and the more anchored you become in your own inner wisdom.

It's not about outsourcing your power to the tool. It's about using the tool to deepen your relationship with your own knowing.

HAVE FUN WITH YOUR MAGIC

You get to have fun with your magic.
Let 'little you' take the reins.
Imagine up scenarios, possibilities.
Let it be playful, limitless, expansive, out of this world.
Make a game of it for yourself.

Remember – you get to have fun with your magic!

EMBODIED MAGIC

Your words are spells.
Your touch is healing.
Your feelings are portals.
Your dreams are visions and guidance.

Your spirit knows the blueprint for your life.
Your bones are grown from the riches of Gaia.
Your blood is made up of waters from the galaxies.
Your cells are encoded with the wisdom of your ancestors.

You are literally magic embodied.
A miracle in human form.
Anything is possible.
If you just remember this.

But the memories run deep.
They are fused into your bones.
The fears are real.
As even to this day, there are those who don't get it.

They tried to discredit you.
They tried to stop you.
They tried to cage you.
They tried to kill you.

But now is not the time to hold back.
You have more power than you were ever led to believe.
It's yours to tap into, harness and wield.
Use for the mission you know you are here for.

You ARE magic embodied.

Remember?

Say it, think it, feel it, know it...

'I AM magic embodied.'

RECEIVING CONSENT

I feel it's important to add in a note here, as someone who has been on the receiving end of unsolicited 'advice' and 'guidance' from people beginning to embody more of their magic and spiritual gifts and bring them into the world.

Please, please seek permission and get approval before using your gifts to read/support/help others. It is not your place to go into their energy field and offer your 'insights', 'wisdom' or anything you might pick up.

I know it is very likely coming from a place of care and wanting to help, or possibly feeling like you are doing them a favour, but don't do it without the individual's consent. Please respect everyone's boundaries and sovereignty here.

Fire: Embodied Leader

I know you are a visionary leader who is carrying a piece of the future. Maybe it's something you haven't fully recognised yet, maybe you haven't named it or welcomed it.

What I know is that you are likely here to lead what hasn't existed yet, which is why you've likely never *really* fit into conventional models.

Your rooted, embodied power is what will support you: to stand in your full truth. To be different. To lean into the unique way you feel, see, hear and receive the world. To show others what's possible. To keep going day-after-day when things get uncomfortable or messy. To do hard things. To believe in yourself when nobody else does. To lead in the way only you can.

This final section includes wisdom and guidance to remind you that you are here to lead in your unique way. There are a number of tools, prompts, stories, reminders and activating codes here to support you. Let yourself receive what you need and trust that whatever that is will be perfect.

MY LEADERSHIP TODAY

When I look at my life today, one of the clearest reflections of how I lead is through the container of my business. It's not just something I do; it's something I am. It's a space I've created from the inside out, rooted in who I am, what I love, and what has shaped me.

This business wasn't something I was taught to build. It didn't come from a textbook or a one-size-fits-all strategy. It has been a slow, intuitive unfolding: a process of remembering, reclaiming and choosing to trust myself again and again. It has meant stepping into my power before I felt ready, and choosing to believe in the vision that kept calling to me.

It's a space where I get to weave together the threads of my own healing and gifts: working with the body, the wisdom of the chakras, past life and inner child regressions, and creative energies. I help people co-create with their businesses and offerings, treating them as living, breathing energies. I support leaders to return to their embodied wisdom, to lean into their creativity and to show up from a place of alignment and truth.

This is my fifth book, alongside four others and an oracle deck I illustrated and created. Each of these creative expressions have been part of my own leadership journey, evidence of what becomes possible when we stop waiting for permission and start following what's true.

I get to remind people of their own power: to create, to live, to express, to thrive, to lead. I get to hold space for them to become more of their whole, creative, embodied selves. And I know that when they do, the ripple effects move far beyond anything we can track.

Yes, there are visible ways I lead through my work, my words and my creations. But what's often unseen is the depth of inner work it has taken to hold this. The hard choices I've had to make in devotion to my vision. The things I've had to release: relationships, homes, identities that no longer fit. The discomfort of shedding layers I'd outgrown. The grief and the growth. The constant returning to myself, especially in the moments where it would have been easier to give it all up.

This, to me, is the deeper layer of leadership.

It begins in self-responsibility and self-honouring. It asks us to walk our truth, even when it's inconvenient. It asks us to create from alignment, not from performance. And it leads to something far more meaningful than just influence or outcomes: a life and a body of work that is true.

This is the leadership I believe in. One that rises from within, ripples outward and keeps evolving as we do.

WHAT IS LEADERSHIP?

I used to believe leadership meant standing in the spotlight, making an impact in a big, world-changing way: CEOs, political figures, high-profile change-makers. And yes, leadership can look like that. But it's so much more. It's something deeper – something you feel in your bones.

Leadership is presence.
It's how you show up every day – how you care, how you create, how you hold space, for yourself and others.
It's the responsibility you carry, even when no one sees it.
It's the courage to stand up for what you believe in, even if it feels futile or overwhelming.
It's staying true to your beliefs, even when the world pulls you elsewhere.
It's seeing where the rules *must* be broken and a new way forged.
It's the quiet moments of integrity; the decisions made from wisdom rather than fear.
It's respecting the knowing of your body as part of the Earth.
It's showing up to do the work even though you might never see its full impact.
It's staying curious and open, willing to be wrong.
It's being willing to learn, to be and do better.
It's choosing love, again and again.

Leadership isn't about becoming someone else. It's about becoming *more of you.*

In a world facing constant shifts and challenges, where uncertainty often feels present, I see this as an invitation, a call for you to step fully into your leadership. Now, more than ever, your unique way of leading is needed. It's time to answer the call and embrace your power with clarity and purpose.

YOU CAME HERE WITH A FREQUENCY

You arrived encoded with something rare.
A frequency that is yours alone.

What is it that wants to be fully claimed?
What moves through you with ease, so natural, it barely feels like effort?
What is the texture, the tone, the colour, the energy, the essence of it?
What's the medicine, the magic, the transmission that only you hold?

This is your frequency signature: your gift for the world.

The more you attune to it, embody it, amplify it... the less you'll ever feel the need to prove, perform, or compare.

There *is* no competition. Nobody else carries what you do. No one else ever will.

To explore your unique frequency more deeply, I invite you to take a look at my 'Frequency First' mini course. Details are in the Resources section.

THE TIME OF THE VISIONARY, CREATIVE LEADER IS HERE

No more holding back your wise, wild, crazy quirks.
No more playing small, letting others take the credit.
No more pretending you aren't as good as you are.
No more struggling, giving away your gifts for peanuts, unless you truly want to.

It's time to own the unique way you see, feel, hear and receive the world.
It's time to own the energetic frequency only you can transmit.
It's time to claim the gifts that move through you without even trying.
It's time to embody the visionary, creative leader that you KNOW you are.

You'll have to bet on yourself.
You'll have to take risks and chances.
It will likely be messy.
You'll feel out of control.

Know you are so held, guided and supported.
Reach out, ask for help, ask again, and again.
Keep showing up, one step after the next.
Keep reminding yourself that this is why you chose to be here now.

YOU ARE THE FORMULA

When you're here to create a new way, your leadership won't always look like what you've seen before. You won't have a clear template to follow, or a set of steps to lean on. Sometimes, there simply isn't someone who has gone before you – not in the way you are meant to do it. You are the one who goes first.

This can feel disorienting at times. You might look around and not see reflections of yourself or your work. The usual signs that things are working – likes, comments, applause, waiting lists, constant validation – might not show up in the way they do for others. Your audience might be quiet. The response might be slower, more subtle, or look completely different from what the world says is 'normal.'

That doesn't mean it isn't working. It means you are building something that doesn't exist yet.

Your power lives in the way you think, see, sense and create. In how you notice what others miss. In how you connect the dots between things that don't seem connected. In how you hold space for ideas, ways of being, or possibilities that the current world hasn't fully caught up to.

It also means that your journey will look different. You might not grow in linear ways. You might have seasons of deep inward work where nothing looks visible on the surface, followed by sudden waves of momentum that seem to come from nowhere. You might not fit neatly into categories, labels, or systems designed for different ways of working.

The truth is, if you're building a new way, there won't be a formula for it, because *you* are the formula. Your presence, your way of holding vision, your way of moving through the world, is what creates the path.

This is what visionary leadership often looks like behind the scenes. It's not always loud or widely recognised at first. It's not always met with instant feedback or external confirmation. But that doesn't make it any less powerful.

It asks you to trust what you know. To keep holding the vision even when it feels like no one else fully sees it yet. To stay grounded in your own rhythm, your own creative intelligence, your own inner knowing.

Because that *is* the way.

THE LEADER'S JOURNEY

This journey will be messy.
It will pull you down.
Make you wonder why you signed up for this.
Think that nobody else gets it.
You'll think it's not for you.
You'll question your worth.
Think you'll never make a difference

But, keep holding the faith.
Keep connecting to your vision.
Trust your guidance, your gifts, your magic.
Let the non-physical hold you.
Trust that what you bring is needed by others.

Let it be messy. Up and down, all over the place.
Support yourself immaculately.
Do what it takes to heal, grow and evolve.
Have fun along the way.
Hang out with those who get it.

Keep showing up.
Taking it one step at a time.
Keep backing yourself, no matter the outcome.
Keep believing in yourself.
Keep choosing yourself.

DISRUPTORS, REBELS AND CHANGE-MAKERS

If you are a visionary you are already a disruptor, rebel and change-maker. Often people hear these identifiers and think they're for activists, people on the front-lines, those making headlines, lots of noise.

But what about the visionary quietly creating a rebellion of self-love.
The environmentalist who works with women to up-cycle discarded clothes and glassware, which they can now sell.
The artist shifting the energy of a room with her multi-dimensional, galactic paintings.
The writer who weaves truth through fiction, awakening memories in those who read between the lines.
The coach who models radical rest in a culture addicted to hustle.
The entrepreneur who chooses integrity over algorithms, intimacy over scale.
The healer who reclaims her ancestral wisdom and quietly rebuilds a lineage of abundance.
The mother who raises her children with reverence for their intuition, breaking generational patterns with every choice she makes.
The leader who listens more than they speak, and moves at the pace of inner alignment instead of fear.

These are the new disruptors, rebels and change-makers to me.
Change woven through everyday choices.
Not always loud, but deeply felt.

Your frequency is your activism.
Your embodiment is your leadership.
Your creativity is your change-making.

BRIDGING THE WORLDS

You don't *really* fit in, because you were never meant to.
You are here to be a bridge between worlds.
A channel between the mystical and the grounded.
A multi-dimensional being grown from layers of wealth.

The hardest part can be bridging the two.
Sharing your gifts in ways that are received.
Bringing miracles into the mundane.
Reminding others of riches unseen by the naked eye.

You have masked it well.
You have numbed, dulled and adapted to try and belong.
But through this you lost the true power of you.
The essence you are as a connector of worlds.

It's time to re-kindle this knowing.
Nurture the parts of you that got abandoned.
Call upon your magic.
Root into the Earth.

Be here fully.
Be you fully.

EMBRACE THE PARADOX

I've often felt like a walking paradox.
Sensitive and fiery. Scattered and laser clear.
Deep in the mystery and still embodied in my knowing.
It used to confuse me, this feeling of being all over the place and yet completely anchored in something undeniable.
I felt like I wasn't allowed to be both.

But that confusion? It wasn't mine.
It was a reflection of a world that told me I had to be one thing.
Clear or messy. Artistic or successful. Strategic or intuitive.
Pick a lane. Be consistent. Fit into a box.
Fuck that.

I'm done trying to make myself make sense in a world that flattens truth into either/or.
I've always held the both/and.
Always been the contradiction.
I'm just no longer hiding it.
It's not confusion, it's capacity.
It's not inconsistency, it's complexity.

And maybe this is the revolution: to stop explaining ourselves and just be it.

So yes, I can feel completely out of it and still know exactly what I'm here for.
I can cry my eyes out one moment and channel clarity in the next.
I can be a vulnerable mess and a powerful guide.
And I've learned how to hold it all without losing myself.

SOFTENING INTO YOUR POWER AS A GENTLE LEADER

The world has mostly taught us that business requires consistency: being 'on' even when it doesn't feel right... bold (or at least loud)... compartmentalised (emotions stay hidden)... and willing to push through at all costs.

As a naturally sensitive, gentle leader, you've probably mastered the art of adapting, masking parts of yourself to fit the status quo. But it's likely left you feeling deeply conflicted inside.

You know how to 'turn it on' and get things done. But your inner, cyclical nature is screaming that this way is not meant for you.

You've likely built a layer of armour to shield yourself from the harshness of it all. Some days, it's the only thing holding you up. It might even feel like you've been carrying it for lifetimes – almost forgetting how to take it off.

The softer, curious, playful part of you has been hiding since childhood, tucked away when it comes to work. It might show itself with close friends or after a few drinks, but rarely feels safe in leadership or business spaces.

Your tender, intuitive nature has been questioned, dismissed, or brushed aside. You *want* to trust it, but it often doesn't align with how the world expects things to work.

Yet... this is your true power.

The very parts the world hasn't welcomed – *these* are your gifts as a leader. Gifts that serve those you're here for in ways no strategy, plan, or 'how-to' ever could.

When you come back into your heart... into your body... deep into your sacral and your root... you reclaim your wholeness. You begin melting away the layers of conditioning, the shoulds, the have-tos: everything you were taught but never truly aligned with.

When you quiet the noise and drop into the softness of your being, you remember your truth.

In this space, you hold and heal the hurts, the stories, the memories – the places still gripping on. And you hear the deep wisdom of your body, guiding you home to your true leadership power.

You remember you are here to lead in a way that is cyclical, softer, magical, playful, flowing and deeply aligned. You feel how *right* this way is – and that you are here to embody your whole self in *every* area of life.

You re-connect to your unique essence, your life-force, your sexual energy, which is pure creative potential. From this you can tap into more pleasure and passion, as you feel the sensuality of being in a body. A body that is designed to feel, and from this feeling it creates.

It's a feeling... a knowing... a remembering that anything is possible and you are powerful beyond belief! Not because you have done something, or shown up in a certain way.

It's a power that comes from deep within, from receiving all of you.

It's the power of being you.

LETTING THE MYSTERY LEAD

So many leaders in business, in my experience, lead in a way that is rooted in the capitalist, patriarchal systems that dominate. Even if on the outside they are championing feminine flow, intuitive leadership, cyclical ways of creating, they are doing it in a system that is inherently not built for the sheer magnificence of the feminine mystery. Behind the scenes there's often pushing, forcing, trying to make things happen. Constant pursuit of growth. Fear of stopping in case you fall behind. Seeing every person you meet as a potential client or lead for your funnel. I get it. I've done it myself. It's the way that we've all been taught to do it, it's the way that we've been taught to measure success by.

I'm sure I don't need to tell you all the issues that this way of working, leading and being in the world has caused: burnout, inequality and over-consumption, to name a few.

However, I believe that if you are here to lead in a new way, you have to begin to do things that truly honour the nature of the feminine. Yes, the masculine energy is needed to hold the feminine, so She feels supported, held and safe. This might come from within – such as a connection with your inner masculine energy. Or it might come from the holding of a team, mentor, a partner even – someone who holds you unconditionally.

(I refer to the feminine and masculine energies here, which have nothing to do with gender but are both present in all of us.)

When the feminine energy is held by the masculine in leadership, She can change the world. She is embodied power.

It begins by connecting to Her frequency – which is a part of you. Honouring Her. Feeling Her. Letting Her lead. She will show you the way. Trusting this can be the hardest part – as it doesn't follow a linear timeline, pattern or way.

It will look like:

Letting go of timelines, strategies, offerings, identities: anything that no longer fits.
Learning to sit in the void. Often. Letting the void become your co-creator.
Trusting the unseen. Trusting your own energetic blueprint.
Valuing rest, play, pleasure, creativity and softness, not as an afterthought but as strategy.
Prioritising frequency over formula. Alignment over hustle.
Choosing to move in cycles, not straight lines.
Disappointing others rather than betraying yourself.
Letting yourself be the signal, not the seeker.
Being willing for your income, your impact and your visibility to be seasonal, cyclical, non-linear.

This is not the easy path.
It will stretch you.
It will ask you to choose yourself, again and again, over the expectations of others, over the conditioning that still lives in your cells.

But if you let the mystery lead, if you *really* keep letting this be the way, I have a feeling you'll receive more magic and miracles in your life than you could ever believe possible. Your leadership will flow, and you'll feel so much more ease and joy-full than ever before.

If you want to begin to connect back into your feminine frequency: Her wisdom, and a way that is rooted in who you truly are, check out the Resources section at the end. I have a number of ways to do this as it's something I am deeply passionate about. In particular take a look at the 'Claim your Creativity' free experience, and the 'Frequency First' mini (but potent) course.

WHAT IF YOU COULDN'T GET IT WRONG?

This is a question that has freed myself and many clients from the overwhelming procrastination and fear that keeps you stuck, playing small, not doing the thing and perpetuating the systems that currently exist.

It ultimately comes down to judgement of what is right and what is wrong. Morality, and fear of consequences – whether real or perceived. Or fear that if you do one thing you'll miss out on what might happen if you'd chosen the other thing.

Please don't get me wrong, I know there are things we can do that can of course create horrific outcomes and that might feel like you have done something wrong. But in most cases I am talking about making a choice, or doing something, where this is not likely going to be the case.

So, rather than trying to figure it all out, trying to control every step (which I am sure if you are here, you already know you can't), stop wading in perfection, over-analysing, and just do the thing. Make a choice, take the action – and know you can't get it wrong!

No matter what you decide to do, the journey will take your life on a trajectory that will give you an experience that will likely grow and expand you in some way.

Trust what you are being called to do. Who you are being called to be. Trust you are guided and supported.

TUG OF WAR

You're loitering at the edges. Between what you know and what you really *know*.
The place where you *know* you need to go, and all will change forever.
But you haven't quite let go, as the other place is familiar, a weighted blanket, the better known.
Society tells you to stay there, draws you back in with its deceptive allure of safety, security.

But when did you ever really fit there? Feel at home there? Actually belong?
You know you don't. You know you are here to be free, wild, unbound.
So stop peeking over the edges, one foot in, one foot out.
This tug of war is caging you on a battlefield of your own making.

You have to choose to trust what you *know*.
You have to decide it now.
Go on.
You know.

IT'S NEVER GOING TO BE PERFECT

This journey is messy, it's imperfect; we're all stumbling along together. You will mess up, make mistakes, change your mind, look back and think *'WTAF was I thinking back then, who WAS that person?!'*

I let the imperfection hold me back for a long time. I know many do.

We are so trained to believe that things have to look or feel a certain way before we take action – put ourselves out there.

As a leader of the new, you are literally bringing in things that we've likely never seen in our lifetimes (especially not in the way only *you* can).

So I invite you to embrace this.
Trust the imperfection as a part of the journey.

You are always in process.
You are always becoming.

KNOW WHEN IT'S TIME TO LET GO

I include this as it's come up a lot for myself and the leaders I have worked with. It's so easy to want to hang on to things – like offers, clients, ways of being and doing, programmes you are in – the list is endless!

It's so important to release things when you *know* the energy is no longer there. When you know it's time to move on. To let things go with love.

I know this can feel scary – there's comfort in the known, layered with pseudo-control, or fear that nothing will replace it.

But, if you learn to let go, to trust this when it comes up, you'll free up so much energetic space for the new – for what's aligned to and for you next.

Yes, there might be a period of emptiness, a void, a messiness while things shift and re-arrange. But trust, believe, have faith that something even better is coming. From my experience it always will.

WHEN YOU ENTER THE VOID

When you work, live and lead in alignment with the seasons, cycles and rhythms of nature, you will naturally find yourself in a void at some point or another. I've found myself in many, each varying in nature.

One of my earlier voids as a business leader was for a few months, just after I had released my first book, *Embodied*, out in to the world. I thought this time would be a bustling period of activity promoting my book, sharing more, working with more people, creating new offers in my business. But nope. Everything dried up. My own energy was low. I felt a wall whenever I tried to create something or do something. So I surrendered and stopped trying to do things. I had some part-time work to keep me going. It felt like everything I had created was crumbling beneath the surface. It was. My first business dissolved, and in its place arrived the business I have today.

Spending time in the void, the space-in-between, is something that we are literally conditioned against. If you aren't do-ing something you aren't being productive. You are missing opportunities. You are missing out on clients. You are missing out on something. People will forget who you are. And. And. And.

But, there is so much power in the void. The letting go of the shoulds, the have-tos, the musts, the expectations. Letting it all fall away, and letting yourself BE in the space before what's coming has arrived.

Here are four things that I was reminded of and that supported me in a longer year-long void, which started beginning in late 2022.

THERE WILL BE SOME UPS AND DOWNS

If you're like me, you might want to burn it all down. Declare it's over. I may have a yin presence, but underneath lives a fire that loves action. So when nothing seemed to land, and my efforts felt pointless, I had to remember: this was incubation. Rest. Integration. Yes, it might last longer than we'd *allow* ourselves. Yes, you might still have immediate needs, like food on the table. But trusting that the wave will rise again, even when you're in the depths of it all, is what carries you through.

BE PRESENT

When things in your business go into a winter, or more inward period, there is an opportunity for more presence in your life. Maybe that's with your partner, children, friends and family. Maybe it's in nature and with your creativity. Maybe it's just with yourself, to be present with what is rising within, with your body, with the emotions that need space. My year in the void felt like about three years to me, which, looking back, I adore (isn't life 'supposed' to speed up and go way too fast) and one of the things I attribute that to is being more present than I have ever been before.

SUPPORT IS LIFE CHANGING

I worked with a coach through it all. She initially came in to support my business, but it was entering winter. I could easily have said I didn't need the support, but I'm happy I prioritised that container over other expenses. She held me. She *saw* me. She understood the sacredness of stillness, the necessity of waiting. We did energy work. We made space for what was becoming (which I now realise was the whispers of this book – *Embodied Power!*). Having that support reminded me not to resist the process, but to trust it.

KEEP HOLDING THE FAITH

Know that the winter/void/space in-between (whatever it feels like to you) WILL end. Things will realign and turn into what they are going to be, if you surrender into this knowing. When you let yourself truly be where you are, what emerges is more beautiful, magical and aligned than anything you could have planned.

RECEIVING FROM THE VOID

These days I love spending time in the void. Sinking deep into my body, into places where I can be beneath the noise of the world. The constructs. The shoulds. The musts. The doing. The expectations.

We all need to be held in the stillness. Being held here to fully, fully let go is, without question, P-O-W-E-R-FULL.

Your nervous system relaxes. Replenishment is received. Alignment with your heart, your soul, your truth is felt... Creation comes from this place. New ideas are born. Clarity on your next step arrives.

When you surrender to it, you unlock alchemy.

SEEKING EXTERNAL VALIDATION

I threw my arms downs as I plopped onto the curb, tears streaming down my face. My partner did his best to hold me as I spiralled into a self-deprecating rant, totally not giving a shit what anyone walking by thought. I was utterly useless. I couldn't make it work. Why didn't anyone want to pay me? I was giving, giving, giving, getting nothing in return.

I had just completed a free online experience taking participants through five sessions of visualisations, journeying to connect with the soul of their business, expanding into the energetics, taking action from a place of alignment. Work I deeply value and know can help. But nobody had taken the next paid step with me and I was charging less than I ever had. I felt depleted, not enough – and yet again wanted to throw it all away.

I knew something had to change. This wasn't my first meltdown when I hadn't been received, and I knew it wouldn't be the last if I didn't stop seeking validation in others.

It goes all the way back to trying to earn approval from teachers, peers, adults, parents – and absorbing messages that my worth was tied to what I produced, how well I performed, or how enthusiastically others responded.

I know this need for external validation is layered. I also know we are hard-wired to want to belong, so we don't end up separate from the pack, and so being approved of is key.

Sound familiar?

We've been conditioned to believe we're only thriving if we're growing, earning, scaling. The metrics of "success" are almost always tied to more: more sales, more clients, more visibility... more, more, more.

It's been a super intentional (and ongoing) journey to heal some of my childhood wounds around this. Going back to meet the younger version of me who needed validation and love.

I don't think the desire to be validated is ever going to go away - or is something to get rid of - after all, I am human. But learning to validate myself, choose myself, back myself is definitely the new baseline I am operating from.

These days I also really value these more subtle signs of success:

- Feeling more at home in my body
- Creating from joy, not pressure
- Saying 'no' when my body says no
- Showing up because I want to, not because I'm chasing validation
- Reclaiming the parts of myself that were silenced, shamed, or dismissed
- Being more present with myself and my loved ones
- Making choices in my business that honour the Earth, even if they take more time or bring in less money
- Uplifting others through my work, even if it isn't measurable in likes, sales, or applause

YOUR CIRCLE OF SUPPORT

Do you have people on this journey with you that get it? That get the journey you are on, and support you? It's all well and good having your parents be a support (and amazing if they are), but unless they are on this journey too, they likely don't understand what it takes.

Having other leaders (whether in a structured container or as friends) you can talk to, receive support from, give support to, and just simply vent to sometimes, can make all the difference.

Having an awesome coach, guide or mentor is highly recommended. Someone you resonate with, someone who really listens to you – and encourages and activates you to take action in ways that work for you. Also acknowledging there'll be times when you may not need this active an approach.

I also really lean on my non-physical support these days. I spend a lot of time talking to, or journaling with, my guides, dragons and the soul of all my creations (books, business, offers, art).

Another thing I do a lot is hand things over to the Universe. This is basically the practice of writing down what you want the Universe to take care of for you. Sometimes I do this on little pieces of paper which I then put into a box and forget about (as it's about trusting the Universe will take care of these things for you).

You can literally do this with anything. Maybe it's something you want clarity around. You could hand over some of the specifics on something you want to happen, which are taking up too much head space. The Universe might then send you guidance on something you could lean into more deeply, someone you could contact, or basically whatever your next aligned step is. It often comes when you least expect it, through magical nudges, signs or symbols.

The one thing I have noticed with this practice is that the things the Universe does take care of for me have not come from my ego (such as numbers of people I want to join an offer I put out). But I do believe anything is possible, so if you do this and that's what is aligned to hand over – then go for it!

TRUST THE PACE OF YOUR BECOMING

I know you are a visionary, a leader, a creative with a mission. You want to do what you love, help people in a way that moves your heart, and make money without feeling like you have to pretend to be someone else, or that your soul is stifled.

I GET this, and am here for it.

But if you're anything like me, there are moments when this path can feel sloooow. When doubt creeps in, whispering that you should be further along by now. You see the overwhelming messages on social media saying you should be making consistent five-figure-plus months. You question if it will *ever* become what you dream of having.

But what if your leadership, your business, your creative body of work, is moving at the exact pace it needs to?

What if the way it's unfolding is part of its strength?

Leadership built on soul alignment, depth, and impact takes *time*.

It takes time to nurture genuine connections – the kind that aren't transactional but rooted in trust and resonance.

It takes time to connect with the right people for your work, the ones who will *get* you, who will resonate with the energy of your message and are here for the profoundly life-changing work you offer.

It takes time to build sustainably – so that your work supports you energetically, financially and creatively over the long term, not just in quick bursts of momentum.

Nature doesn't rush a tree into full bloom before its roots are deep enough to hold it. The same is true for your work. Some seasons are for planting seeds. Some for tending. Some for resting in the unknown. And some for the harvesting.

This is the foundation of embodied leadership.

It's not about forcing, looking for the next gimmick, guru or hack to beat the algorithm. Watering down your message (and what you *really* do) to fit into a neat little box, that cuts out half your heart.

It's about allowing. Growing strong, deep roots into rich, fertile soil. It's about co-creating with the energy of your work in the world. Honouring and holding space for the fullness of who you are, your multi-dimensionality, your paradoxes, your desire for freedom and need to feel safe.

So if you're feeling impatient, take a breath.

Trust that every connection, every iteration, every aligned step is adding to the foundation of something truly sustainable and lasting.

THE POWER OF ENERGETIC CONTAINERS

Having been in many groups and one-to-one containers, from inner child healing to book-writing programmes, I know the power of support. It's an energetic container. In one-to-one spaces, it's someone holding and guiding me to go deeper. In groups, it's the shared intention and energy of everyone inside, with the facilitator anchoring the space.

I'll be honest, I often shied away from groups because I *feel so much*. I didn't want to sit in spaces where I'd be absorbing everyone's stuff as we journeyed together. What I later realised was the power of the *energetics* holding those spaces.

The groups where I felt drained were usually not held well: lacking boundaries, becoming a dumping ground for unprocessed energy that required more attention and left the space feeling all-over-the-place. But the ones that *were* held powerfully had a completely different frequency. They allowed me to soften, let go, be vulnerable, and also see that (often, not always) if something triggered me, it was an invitation to meet and heal something within myself.

Every container, whether group or one-to-one, offers an energetic holding and activation, whether you're consciously aware of it or not. Sometimes, simply by saying *yes,* things start shifting… aligning with the very intention that called you in.

WHAT IF BEING FULLY YOU IS KEY?

What if leadership isn't about compartmentalising, making pieces of you more palatable, but instead about bringing your whole, multi-passionate, unique self to the table?

Not just the efficient manager one. Not just the spiritual one. Not just the people-pleaser.
Not the one you think they want.

But the *you* that feels like truth. Like YOU.

I used to shape-shift, wearing labels like socks: the foodie, the artist, the organiser, the creative.

But underneath, I was always more.

And when I stopped editing my essence, life, love and business shifted. It became what I always wanted. What I'd secretly dreamed of.

Now I lead from wholeness: creative, cosmic, structured, AND soft.

And it works, not in spite of this, but *because* of it.

What if being fully you is the real power you've been waiting to claim?

GETTING TO KNOW THE LITTLE LEADER INSIDE

There's likely a young part inside of you that can show you *more* of the leader you are here to be. And if you are already showing up as a leader I bet they can share more fun, magical, playful parts that make your leadership even richer. That remind you that *you too* are here to bring more fun, magic, miracles and play into your leadership.

The offering here is to tune into this, connecting within, and trusting whichever younger version of you appears and what they might have to say to you.

This is what came for me:

I know my inner leader is rooted in five-year-old me. She is feisty and fiery, loves to wear red and to paint her nails bright pink. She's a powerful creator. She knows what she wants and she creates it effortlessly. She sees things vividly and isn't afraid to speak her mind. She was comfortable being the centre of attention and would happily get up on stage, do public speaking, win competitions, get cast as the lead in plays.

She was often called a bossy boots, judged by others – especially older women whom she could feel disdain dripping from. So she began to dim, hide, pretend she didn't know so much. She began to ignore the wisdom she embodied; it didn't feel safe to trust anymore, as it often got dismissed.

As I strengthened my connection with her, she let me know she wanted to be allowed out to play. She wanted me to wear red and pink again. She told me I needed to stand tall, proud of who I am.

She reminded me I am capable of anything and everything. I needed to believe in myself again and didn't need anyone to validate it for me.

Spending time with her helped me to bring more pleasure and play into my business. She taught me that these qualities have just as much power as taking action in logical ways. These qualities are part of my super power and when I include them in my leadership things flow magically, opportunities align and above all it feels good! And isn't that the whole damn point?!

Update: as I listened and gave space to the little leader inside me, and even other younger versions of me, over time they slowly started to disappear, almost fading away into the background. It felt like they were becoming integrated, their gifts a part of my wholeness, my power, my embodied leader. I can still call on them if I want, but they aren't pulling at me for my attention. They are me; I am them.

WHAT'S STOPPING YOU?

You came here to be a beacon, a light that shines so brightly – as you know you are made of stardust.

You have gifts, talents, qualities, quirks, facets, pieces to a puzzle, that are magically magnificent and uniquely yours.

You knew this when you got here, when you first landed into the physical.

But over time you slowly tried to forget.

The way you can hear the words of the unseen.
The way the Earth speaks through your bones.
The awareness you can project into other dimensions.
The way colours speak to you through their vibration.
The way angels and dragons look out for you.

These qualities, these senses so open to receiving *everything*, were not acceptable, not welcome. So you did what you could to disown them.

To forget they were ever a part of you.

To forget they were a part of your power; a part of what makes you, you.

But what if it's up to you, to make it mainstream. To claim your crazy. To claim it as cool.

What's stopping you?

WHEN THE CRITICS COME OUT

As you begin to step into your power and bring more of your full self into the world, you may experience a whole host of things coming from others who don't want to see you in this way. It could be a shitty off-hand remark, something dismissive or even outright criticism or anger directed at you. You'll likely also *feel* things: someone you thought supported you being silent, someone subtly competing with you.

So this is your reminder that not everyone is ready for you, and you are not for everyone.

I find that connecting back into the energy of my power (you can see more on how to do this in the Power section at the beginning of the book), and the me that fully owns her power, often helps anchor me back into my truth. I do this, and then reflect:

When I connect to this energy, how do I feel?

What does this version have to say to me?

Often it's easy to simply let it go, but if not there might be some inner work to do.

Maybe it's a trigger that's pointing to something deeper, which needs healing, or is an invitation to look at something in a new way. Maybe it's an illustration of just how powerful you are.

It could signal some more nervous system support is needed. Remember you are human and it's okay to take your time to respond to things, feel them, let them out, comfort and support your body to adjust.

Above all, the more and more I embody my power fully, the easier it gets to keep walking the path, to be myself, to show up again and again, no matter how its received.

SMALL ACTS OF CARE

You're someone who leads with heart: thoughtfully, empathetically and with deep intention. So this may go without saying. But in a world that feels increasingly fast-moving and fragmented, it can be hard to keep pace with the ever-evolving nuances of allyship and inclusivity.

I'm not here to position myself as an expert in this space. I'm still learning, unlearning and doing my best to grow. I imagine you are too.

Still, I've noticed a few seemingly small gestures that have had a profound impact on how I've felt seen, considered and included. And perhaps they'll offer you a moment to reflect on how you show up for the people you're here to lead.

Like when a coach includes call times in multiple time zones, acknowledging those of us outside the default.

Or when someone remembers the seasons aren't the same across hemispheres, and honours the energetic shift happening globally, not just locally.

Or when someone is mindful of holidays and observances beyond the mainstream, honouring that not everyone shares the same cultural calendar.

These acts might seem minor. But to me, they're moments of care. They speak to a deeper kind of leadership, one that listens, pays attention, and dares to be human.

We all have bigger causes, values and missions we're championing. We can't do it all, and we're not meant to. But I believe it's the small, often overlooked gestures that quietly shape the most powerful and inclusive spaces. The ones where people feel safe enough to show up fully.

And that changes everything.

EMBODIED VISIBILITY

As a leader, you're likely being called to be visible in some way, to reach or connect with the people you're here to work with. That's not always the case, of course, and if it's not your current path, this piece probably isn't for you.

I've spent a decade working in PR and marketing, followed by over a decade as an entrepreneur. Visibility has been a central thread in my journey. I learned early on that visibility was a numbers game. You had to show up no matter how you felt. It had to be consistent, across every platform you could find your people on, and done in a certain way.

And yes, that approach *does* work for many. But not for me.

Put simply, it's an approach rooted in the patriarchal model of doing business.

I tried to follow it, with varying levels of success – both internal and external. Here's what surfaced, particularly around social media visibility:

- I'd see growth and results when I was sharing regularly (sometimes a few times a day) sending out e-letters, guest posting, pitching for PR exposure, plus running online events. Doing alllll the things I knew to do. And then I'd hit a wall of exhaustion and want to retreat completely, deleting everything.
- If I wasn't receiving positive feedback, I felt pressured to come up with something new or expose my vulnerabilities just to create connection.

- I'd go through highly creative, flowing bursts of expression... which would then dry up, leaving me with the urge to disappear again.
- And of course, I fell into the comparison trap. When others said similar things and received more validation or praise, I felt not enough.

As you can see, my relationship with visibility felt like feeding a hungry ghost. Probably not too dissimilar to yours – these platforms are designed to be constantly fed.

So, I had to find another way. A way of being visible (especially as I've mostly been a solopreneur) that felt sustainable. A way that felt *good* in my body. That honoured my creative flow, my hormonal rhythms, and ultimately allowed me to just be *me*.

It's still evolving. I've experimented with different styles and teachings. I've learned from others and tried a lot of things. But more recently, I've decided to say, *'fuck it'* and do what I want, when I want, and trust that it's more than enough.

I needed to trust myself again. To have *fun* with it. (I also regularly speak to versions of little me to get their take on this!)

So now, there are times when I'm sharing all the time, overflowing with creative energy. And then there are times when I retreat and go inward.

That part hasn't changed – but the *energy* behind it has. Now it's coming from a place of intention, joy and choice. From listening to my body. Not from burnout, depletion or force.
I've also learned, from trial and error, that when I push myself to share from a place of fear (especially needing money to come in), it doesn't land. People can feel the energy. Nothing connects. Zero results.

So now, I'd rather not post at all than push something out just to tick the box. That's hard, by the way. We've been deeply conditioned to believe we must be "on" all the time – or we're failing.

As I write this AI has become a tool to use in the entrepreneurial world, especially for marketing, and I have dabbled with it. It's very useful as a tool for re-purposing or editing the flow of pieces I have already written, so that my energy can go into more creative things, which are my zone of genius. That said, I deeply value human creativity and have concerns about its environmental impact, so I only use it sparingly.

Also, when I first started using AI experimenting with longer pieces, I noticed my brain got... lazy. A friend described it as becoming "less stretchy," and that's *exactly* how it felt. And that's not something I want. I'm here for optimal health, creativity, vitality and for my body to feel *even better* as I age.

Ultimately, embodied visibility is about learning to trust yourself, which is what all of this is really about.

Trusting how and where you want to show up.
When you want to show up.
What you love (and don't love) doing.
Speaking and sharing what you *actually* want to say.
Checking in with your body.
Checking in with the spirit of your work and with what wants to be shared.
Letting your frequency lead.

It's about approaching it all with curiosity. Letting it be a process. An unfolding. Something you get to enjoy.

Something that will likely take longer than the traditional, linear ways, but will feel *so* much better.

At least, I think so.

If this resonates, I have a number of ways you can go deeper into this in the Resources section at the end. In particular, the free 'Claim your creativity' experience.

HOW ARE YOU BEING CALLED TO SHARE?

Less listening to every marketing or sales 'guru' and more sharing YOUR truth and wisdom.

Less doubting your inner wisdom and messages, and more sharing it. Even if it is not for everyone. *Especially* if it is not for everyone.

Less feeling like what you have to share or offer isn't enough. More knowing what a gift you truly are and how you are SO needed at this time.

Less comparing yourself with others and where they are at in their journey. More believing in yourself and trusting that you are on the right path for you.

Less thinking you don't know enough or aren't enough, and more aligning yourself with what you are here to share.

I believe that we're not meant to do it one way, that there is a new way emerging, one that honours creativity, softness, rest and the cyclical creative process.

As a creative visionary you are here to create and lead that way.

You will never be for everyone and even trying to be will only lead to incongruence within.

What are you being called to share at this time?

What does your heart want the world to know?

How does sharing feel good to you?

How does your body want to show up, create and lead in a way that honours its needs?

YOU CAME HERE TO FREAKING RADIATE

You came here to RADIATE
To disrupt.
To awaken.
To be undeniable.

You're not here to play small.
You're not here to shrink, shape-shift, or dim.

You came with codes.
Gold in your bones.
A frequency that shifts rooms.
A voice that was born to *echo*.

You know this.
You've *always* known this.

But somewhere along the way, you toned it down.
Tried to fit in.
Tried to follow the rules.
Let other people's comfort dictate your brilliance.

That ends now.

Because the REAL you?

The one who creates galaxies with their words,
The one who channels power through their presence,
The one who makes *magic* feel like a strategy?
Is ready to lead.

It's time to unleash what's been burning inside you.
To say the thing, share the thing, *sell* the thing.
To make money like a creative force of nature.
To turn your brilliance into something unmissable, unforgettable, unstoppable.

You came here to freaking RADIATE.

EMBODIED IMPACT

I *know* you are here to make an impact in some way.

This word can bring up resistance in some as it definitely has an outward, active energy to it. In one of the groups I run we were diving into the theme of impact and one lovely participant (and friend) was wondering how she can make an impact out in the world, when she's called to tend to her home and garden. This is not an uncommon question. I absolutely feel it's our conditioning telling us that impact has to be outward, tangibly seen, felt or experienced in some way, for it to be of value. For it to have an impact.

But I feel it can be both.

If you are being called to make changes, affect lives and bring your leadership out into the world – that is awesome.

But I also believe impact holds a lighthouse type energy, whereby you impact others simply (yet powerfully) through your presence. Through following what lights you up. Through your devotion to this. This will impact you and your life, which will in turn affect others without you even necessarily noticing it.

One way to re-frame this for yourself, and feel into your embodied impact right now is to connect to the energy of the word. Just invite in the word impact. You could do this by repeating it out loud, in your head, or writing it down. Or you could close your eyes and ask it to come to you as an energy. Then see what it feels like and how you experience it. Ultimately it's about getting your body to experience it and see what arises.

I invite you to try it with openness and curiosity. You might be surprised at what you receive and experience. Also know the guidance might come to you later in some way.

WHO ARE YOU REALLY?

What are your secret desires, that you wouldn't dare let out the safety of your head?

What do you actually care about, but it's not *cool*, or won't make you money, can't be commoditised?

What do you not give a shit about, but pretend to, to keep up appearances? To pander to an outdated identity.

What do you actually want to do with your life – not what you think you should do for your family, your parents, your community – but what do you *really* want to do?

Who do you want to be? What's that secret dream that you locked away in a box after you were told in kindergarten to stop being unrealistic?

What do you wish you could do day in, day out? Where you wake up and go *'fuck yes, this is actually my life.'*

What would you burn to the ground? The stuff that bores the crap out of you. That fills you with dread. That makes you resent it with every inch of your soul.

What would you start nurturing?

What would you start creating?

THIS is the stuff I am here for. I want your wildest, most outlandish ideas. I want the fullest, most outrageous, honest you. I want to know what you feel shame about, what you hide from the world. I want the *real* you, not who the world told you to be.

I want the you who simply is.

This is the stuff that the world needs. This is where the freaking gold is. The magic...

Are you ready to go all in with me?

BECOME THE LEADER YOU ARE HERE TO BE

- What motivates you?
- What are you passionate about?
- What impact are you here to make?
- What have you always wanted to say but haven't?
- What have you always wanted to create?
- What do you wish someone else would do/say/create? *Maybe you are the one to do/say/create the thing.*
- How can you fully embody the leader you are here to be? What will support you? *What would it feel like? What would you be wearing, saying, doing?*
- What are the unique gifts you bring as a leader? What is it time to own about yourself?
- What might you have to let go of? Any habits, behaviours, people, ways or things you know are not supportive.
- How can you show up authentically as a leader?
- Is there anything holding you back in any way from fully embodying the leader you are deep inside?
- What does 'little you' have to say to you about the leader you *really* are here to be?
- What guidance does your body have for you about the leader you are here to be?
- What action are you being invited to take next?

EMBODIED LEADER

Soften into your power.
Nourish your body, mind and soul.
Bring play into your day.
Let pleasure show you the way.

You're here to disrupt the old.
From a place of overflow and abundance.
Bringing dreams down.
To root into the Earth.

Your truth is here to guide you.
Your being-ness is key.
To letting your light shine from within.
To making the impact only you can.

Come back to your wholeness.
Create space to receive all of you.
To step into your leadership.
Become the leader you came here to be.

These themes and ways of becoming an embodied leader are all part of my Embodied Business® Leaders' programme, which you can find details for in the Resources section at the end.

A PORTAL INTO YOUR POWER

Thank you for picking up this book and letting it be a part of your journey. Whether you've dipped in and out, or touched on all the pieces contained within, I hope that you have received: inspiration, magic, deep knowings and rememberings, reminders, activations and codes that will support you to step even more into your power as the visionary leader YOU ARE. You may find that these things continue to activate and happen long after you are finished with these words (that is certainly my intention for you).

Thank you for saying yes to this journey, even if at times you might not want to! It's certainly not the easy path as you are creating new ways, and going against the majority.

Keep going, keep taking one step at a time, day after day.

Keep trusting yourself, your inner wisdom, your guides, your knowing.

Lean on community, love hard, let yourself receive love.

Be kind to yourself, remember you are human!

Keep leading in the way only you can.

LET'S GO DEEPER

Words can only take us so far. Much of what I've shared lives beyond language, in frequency, energy and embodied experience. If something within you feels stirred, a curiosity, a resonance, a knowing, there are ways we can journey deeper together.

Whether you're called to 1:1 or group mentorship, or seeking support for your workplace or leadership path, I'm here to hold that space.

I invite you to book in a complimentary connection call with me to explore what might be possible. You can do that here:

https://calendly.com/tarajackson/.

Also take a look in the Resources section on the following page.

RESOURCES

FURTHER RESOURCES AND WAYS TO CONNECT WITH ME

Ways to go deeper specifically mentioned in the book are all on this webpage (including more up-to-date ways to go deeper as I create them):

https://empathpreneurs.org/embodied-power-book

You can also find them directly below.

Embodied Business® Leaders

A private mentorship for visionary leaders ready to grow their business in alignment with their energy, creativity and deeper truth.
https://empathpreneurs.org/offerings/embodied-business-leaders/

Timeline jumping bundle

Activations to shift your frequency, collapse timelines and step into your next-level reality – now.
https://empathpreneurs.org/product/timeline-jumping/

Claim your creativity

A free experience to reclaim your voice, magic and creative power, on your terms, in your way.
https://embodied-business.teachable.com/p/claim-your-creativity

Frequency First – a mini course for visionary leaders

A self-paced mini-course for visionary leaders ready to lead from frequency, not force – and let their energy do the heavy lifting.
https://empathpreneurs.org/offerings/frequency-first/

MY BOOKS

All available anywhere you buy your books online.

Embodied – A self-care guide for sensitive souls
Embodied Business – A guide to grounding and aligning your business chakras for empathpreneurs
Embodied Creation – The sensitive's way to consciously co-create
Embodied Wealth – I AM

MY ORACLE CARD DECK

Embodied Wisdom – A colour alchemy card deck to bring you into alignment with your truth. Available to purchase at:
https://empathpreneurs.org/product/embodied-wisdom
(limited copies available).

Insight Timer – My meditations and visualisations mentioned throughout the book (including many more, which are updated on a regular-ish basis) are available here:
https://insighttimer.com/love-embodied

Instagram – This is the main social channel I hang out on: https://www.instagram.com/iamtarajackson/

MAIN WEBSITE

You can also get in touch with me if you would like one-to-one or group support (I offer a number of programmes, courses and workshops). You can find me at www.empathpreneurs.org.

My web shop is at https://empathpreneurs.org/shop.

This is my other website to support leaders with writing and the creative process: www.tarajackson.co.uk.

BOOK WRITING AND PUBLISHING FOR VISIONARY LEADERS

Writing this book and stepping more fully into my power inspired the birth of my own hybrid publishing company, **Global Soul Press** – an idea that had been quietly forming for over a year. The finer details are still unfolding, but you can see more and follow the journey on Instagram: https://www.instagram.com/globalsoulpress/

WORKING WITH LIMITING BELIEFS

(A process from my book *Embodied Creation*)

When beliefs come up, the next step is starting to see where they came from, then heal, release, forgive and let them go before beginning to rewrite them. Here is a process you can use for all beliefs.

1. Start to become aware of all the thoughts and ideas coming up telling you that you can't have/embody/bring through what you desire, and the beliefs that you have created. Here are some questions to help you tune into the underlying belief that might be playing out.

    - Why don't you actually want what you say you do?
    - What do you fear you will lose if you get what you desire?
    - What fears are rising?
    - What bad things do you think will happen if you get what you desire?
    - What are all the reasons coming up that tell you that you can't have it/why it's not possible for you?
    - What would having/receiving this mean for you?
    - How would it change your life negatively? (You may not think it will on the surface, but as you dig into it, I am sure you will come up with some reasons.)

2. Now, looking at everything you wrote down, ask yourself, 'Is it true?' (It very rarely is, and if there's an element of truth in there, it is likely not the whole truth and can be shifted, or perhaps you are here to create a new way!)

3. Start to re-write these beliefs. Hold and heal anything that needs to be. Where did it come from? Often we need to go back to childhood and comfort that younger version of ourselves, letting them know that it's okay and even doing some re-parenting. It might also be ancestral, from a past life or conditioning, in which case you may need some other support to let it go.

   Spend time forgiving or releasing anything or anyone that played a part in this belief being formed, for your own sake. Set an intention to release and let those beliefs go, even if it feels like you don't know how yet – the inspiration will come.

4. Connect with these new truths/possibilities and really spend time embodying each one of them wholly – connecting to and feeling it in all of your being.

   More 'stuff' may arise as you begin to connect with new truths/possibilities – these are all the things you need to continue to work through.

OVERVIEW OF THE MAIN CHAKRAS

EARTH STAR CHAKRA (VASUNDHARA)

Your Earth star chakra is located a few inches below your feet and makes up part of your etheric body. It connects directly to the core of the Earth, and as such connects you to it also. It is the grounding point for your entire chakra system and etheric body. It connects you to not only the Earth but the whole of humanity as well. I personally see it as a copper colour.

ROOT OR BASE CHAKRA (MULADHARA)

The root chakra is the area of consciousness of the physical body. It is traditionally seen as the colour red and is located at the base of your spine. It grounds, anchors and supports you as you engage with everyday life.

SACRAL CHAKRA (SVADHISTHANA)

The sacral chakra is located a few centimetres below your belly button and is traditionally associated with the colour orange. It is your creativity centre, connected with your feelings and emotions.

SOLAR PLEXUS CHAKRA (MANIPURA)

The solar plexus chakra is the power centre of your being and is located in the middle of the body a few centimetres above the belly button. It is usually associated with the colour yellow. It is connected to your worth and power as an individual.

HEART CHAKRA (ANAHATA)

The heart chakra is traditionally associated with the colour green and is connected to love, relationships, and your connection with yourself and others.

THROAT CHAKRA (VISHUDDA)

The throat chakra is traditionally associated with the colour blue and is connected to your communication and expression: speaking up and being heard.

THIRD EYE CHAKRA (AJNA)

The third eye chakra, located between your eyebrows, is associated with the colour indigo or royal blue and is connected to your inner wisdom and knowing, your intuition, foresight, vision and decisions.

CROWN CHAKRA (SAHASRARA)

The crown chakra, at the top of the head and skull, is traditionally associated with the colour purple and is connected to higher states of consciousness and a remembrance that we are all part of a greater whole.

SOUL STAR CHAKRA (VYAPINI)

The soul star chakra is around a few inches above the head and is traditionally associated with the colours silver/white and/or magenta. It is a bridge between the physical and the non-physical, and holds the truth of how you individually fit into the bigger picture of humanity and consciousness. It is about integrating the physical and non-physical, to restore your sense of unique life purpose, direction, and place in the greater universe.

CHAKRAS DIAGRAM

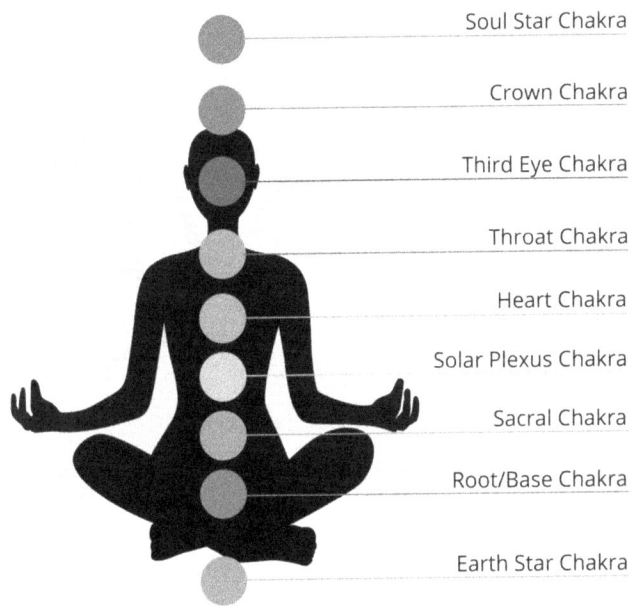

- Soul Star Chakra
- Crown Chakra
- Third Eye Chakra
- Throat Chakra
- Heart Chakra
- Solar Plexus Chakra
- Sacral Chakra
- Root/Base Chakra
- Earth Star Chakra

ACKNOWLEDGEMENTS

There have been so many incredible humans who have contributed to my journey, who've inspired me, held space for me, worked with me, and as such have added to this book in some way. To everyone who has been a part of my journey in any capacity, I thank you deeply.

There are a few people who directly helped me to birth this book:

Robin, thank you for walking alongside me (literally at times), for receiving ALL of me. Thank you for getting it, for getting me, and for all your power-full support and holding – especially through the messiness of it all.

Toni, you are epic! I'm so honoured to walk alongside you. Your holding and wisdom has been the best midwife for *Embodied Power*, and I'm beyond grateful to and for you.

Rachel, thank you for being an incredible coach and guide, and holding me through the beginning whispers of *Embodied Power*, when I didn't even recognise this is what She would turn into.

Bec, thank you for your generous group activations and powerful sessions re-connecting me into my true frequency.

Shannon, working with you was a blessing and gift that helped me remember MY way.

Nicola, (and The Unbound Press team) as always, I am so grateful for all your support. Thank you for paving the way for *this* way of writing in the world. Lovely Em, I'm so honoured and grateful to have you editing my words. And Lynda, thank you for bringing the energy into its magical cover.

ABOUT THE AUTHOR

Tara Jackson is a creativity mentor, visionary guide, and the catalyst behind transformational journeys for leaders, entrepreneurs, and creatives ready to step fully into their power. She helps people reclaim their creative essence, turn bold ideas into reality, and write and publish books that amplify their message and expand their impact.

Blending practical strategy, spiritual insight, and energetic alignment, Tara shows others how to navigate both the inner and outer landscapes of success with courage, clarity, and ease.
Her work invites you to embody your truth, unleash your unique gifts, and create a life and legacy of soulful impact.

She lives between Kenya and the UK, but mostly works with clients online.

www.ingramcontent.com/pod-product-compliance
Lightning Source LLC
Chambersburg PA
CBHW061229070526
44584CB00030B/4050

www.ingramcontent.com/pod-product-compliance
Lightning Source LLC
Chambersburg PA
CBHW061229070526
44584CB00030B/4050